We Must Be Daft!

Best Wishes

We Must Be Daft!

Following The Fortunes Of Dundee FC

Peter Caproni

Think Big Press
www.thinkbigpress.com

Published in the United Kingdom by:

Think Big Press

www.thinkbigpress.com

A catalogue for this book is available from the British Library.

ISBN 978-0-9558599-1-5

Printed and bound in Great Britain by CPI Antony Rowe, Eastbourne

Dedicated to my late Dad,

Tommy Caproni, who introduced me

to Dundee FC

Contents

Foreword

By
Alan Cousin

I first met Peter Caproni in the sixties when I was coaching one night a week at the local Y.M.C.A in Alloa. Peter was one of several youngsters who showed genuine ability, and it was no surprise that he duly made his way into the senior ranks with Stirling Albion and Alloa Athletic.

Although hampered in his playing career by illness and injury, he spent many years coaching and plying his trade as a professionally trained Sports Therapist. However, during over thirty years in the game, his heart and allegiance never strayed far from Dens Park.

This book records in detail what it means to be a dedicated follower of Dundee F.C. over those years; the ups and downs, the elation and the despair, and the heady days of 1962 when the league was won. Then, in the following season, the feverish excitement of those European Cup nights when the unlikely dream seemed so possible! Great days! It's all here. Peter's account revived for me so many happy memories of a thrilling period in the club's history.

Acknowledgements

In writing this book, many hours were spent going through scrap books that I kept as a young boy but also the information and help given by Norrie Price and his publications of "They Wore The Dark Blue" and "Up Wi' The Bonnets" was hugely informative in confirmation of my own recollections of games and years gone by.

I would also like to convey my thanks to D.C. Thomson (Dundee) and in particular Bill McLoughlin for allowing me to reproduce their photographs which will bring back so many memories to all Dundee supporters.

My thanks also, to the Alloa Advertiser and Stirling Observer for allowing me to use photographs of my time at Alloa Athletic and Stirling Albion.

Thanks also are due to Alan Cousin for writing the foreword. Alan was one of the game's gentlemen, and in his long, illustrious career, was never booked, despite being the victim of some horrendous treatment both at home and abroad. I visited Alan recently and in his living room a picture of the Championship winning side takes pride of place. Alan spoke of his time at Dens with great affection for both the club and its supporters. The master of the "double shuffle". A true Dundee legend.

I also must thank my family; my wife, Elma, for putting up with my permanent love of all things Dundee and my two sons, Michael and Mark, who have experienced many of the emotions about which I have written.

Finally, I would like to thank my daughter Elizabeth (Liz, to me). Her constant encouragement and her professional guidance in both content and editing on this book, has been indispensable.

Introduction

Being a Dundee supporter takes a special kind of person, as their volatile form is unsympathetic to your emotions, as I learned from an early age.

I was born in Stirling in 1947 and brought up in the Hillfoots village of Tillicoultry, in Clackmannanshire. I now live with my wife of thirty-eight years, in Sauchie, approximately two miles from my original family home, and fifty-two miles exactly to Dens Park.

My grandmother, from my Father's side, was a Dundonian, and so my Dad brought me up to forsake the "old firm" and follow the fortunes of his Mother's hometown team.

So there I was, aged seven, standing behind the goal for the first game of the season 1954-55, watching in awe as Dundee's goalkeeper, Bill Brown took his first goal kick in front of 30,000 fans at Tynecastle.

That was it - I was hooked for life!

This is the reason why I decided to write about following the fortunes of Dundee in that era. Dundee, then, were incredibly similar to today's team (2009) in regards to their unpredictability – but there was magic back then. The football that was played by the legends Alan Cousin, Alan Gilzean and Jocky Scott was, at times, breathtaking.

If you were around in the fifties to the seventies, this book will bring back a mixture of heartbreaking and absolute glorious memories of the Dundee that was. If, however, you are too young for those memories to be jogged, you will not only see the similarities of the Dundee then and the Dundee now, but you will hopefully also get a glimpse of the sheer brilliance and class that Dundee used to produce......and have you dreaming big for the future.

Chapter 1

Grin And Bear It

I would be around seven years old, and every Sunday morning after Mass, I used to walk to the newsagent, that was once my (Italian) grandfather's Fish and Chip shop. It was then that my Dad used to tell of the glorious times in Dundee's past.

I loved these stories and never tired hearing them; stories of happier days when Dundee were arguably the third force in Scottish football.

However, it was the season 1953-54 before I can honestly say that I took an interest in football (I should probably go easy on myself though as I was only six years old!). It was then that I just knew that I wanted to be a footballer - nothing else mattered, but more on that later.

Sadly, I have no memory of the season before, when Dundee beat Kilmarnock 2-0 to win the League Cup in October 1952. That was their second successive League Cup Final triumph, having beaten Rangers 3-2 the season before with a dramatic last second winner from Alfie Boyd. I cannot recollect that victorious moment but I can tell you exactly how the goal was scored - thanks to my Dad's story telling skills! The legendary Billy Steel placed a free kick, probably lace away, as his cross was so accurate, onto the head of skipper Boyd, who headed home for a glorious winner! (Lace away was a saying in the fifties and sixties when footballs were laced up, and there sometimes was a little knot where the lace was tied. So if you were unlucky enough to head it, it could "gie ye a sare yin"!)

The Rollercoaster Ride Begins!

Early in 1954, Dundee, who had suffered four defeats in their previous five games, were drawn against Albion Rovers of the Second Division, in the Scottish Cup Second Round. I, the youngest of the Caproni household, sat eagerly awaiting the result on the *Home Service*, which at that time was probably the nearest thing there was to *Radio Scotland.* "Albion Rovers 1, Dundee 1". OK, I thought, we will sort them out at Dens - and we did - by four goals to nil! George Merchant, who had scored our goal on the Saturday at Coatbridge, scored all four at Dens, one penalty included.

I was excited now. Who will we get in the next round? Please, God, I prayed, don't make it Celtic or Rangers. My prayers were apparently heard. It was Rangers but of a different sort - Berwick Rangers.

The "wee" Rangers plied their trade in the "C" Division which was in the main made up of reserve sides from the "A" Division, which was the top division in these days. So, hardly - on paper any way - stiff opposition.

"Dundee will beat them Dad!" I exclaimed, looking for some assurance from my Father.

"You never know with Dundee son," Dad replied and so I wondered, even at that young age, why my Dad should be so unsure. I was soon to be enlightened. Travelling to Berwick to see the match would have been out of the question as at that time we didn't have a car, so I listened with bated breath for the result on the radio. Berwick Rangers 3, Dundee 0. My little, naïve mind was ever so troubled!

The astonishing thing was that the Dundee team that day had amazing players in their line up; Doug Cowie, a Scottish International and one of Dundee's all time greats, goal keeper Bill Brown, who would go on to play for his country, Tommy Gallacher, who just oozed class, and the legendary Billy Steel, arguably

Dundee's greatest ever player (Billy had represented a side chosen from all the great players in Europe to play against a "Rest of the World" team and who had cost a Scottish record transfer fee!).

"Don't let it worry you," my Dad said, as he hugged me goodnight, "We'll come again." And with that firmly wedged in my mind, I trudged solemnly to bed.

Dundee's form in the next six games was chequered to say the least; three wins, two defeats and a draw. Going into the last game of the season against third placed high-flying Partick Thistle, the Dark Blues sat comfortably in seventh spot in the table. Even though the game was at Dens, to say I didn't fancy our chances is an understatement. But Dad was right - Dundee "came again".

Dundee 6, Partick Thistle nil. Dundee WERE a great team after all. Why had I been so worried?

Chapter 2

A Light At The End Of The Tunnel

August 14th 1954, Tynecastle Park

Hearts 3 - 1 Dundee

There was great excitement in the Caproni household when Dad announced that we were going to go to the first game of the season! Hearts versus Dundee at Tynecastle. My *very first* game watching my beloved Dark Blues! I had badgered Dad for ages to take me to a game but the season before he probably thought that I was still too young. So this season couldn't come quickly enough!

My distant memory of the game at Tynecastle was standing behind the goalposts, watching Dundee's goalkeeper, Bill Brown, about whom my Dad had told me so often, take a goal kick. It was almost surreal. Although we lost 3-1, strangely, however, I cannot recall feeling down about losing. The excitement of the day and actually seeing Bill Brown in the flesh probably had something to do with it!

As we didn't have a car, opportunities to see Dundee in action were scarce, and it was to places like Falkirk - which was only about fifteen miles from our home in Tillicoultry - that provided us with the best chance of seeing Dundee play. Watching them occasionally in the flesh, however, provided me with early evidence that supporting the "Dark Blues" was not going to be a bed of roses.

The League Cup competition in these days consisted of mini leagues of four clubs, the winner of which would progress to the next round. The 'Dee, unfortunately, got off to a bad start, losing at Tynecastle. However, they soon got on a winning streak; beating Champions Celtic 2-1 at home in front of 29,000, which was a terrific result. Falkirk were beaten 3-1, and then, before a crowd of 30,000 at Dens, the Dark Blues thumped Hearts 4-1. They then travelled to Celtic Park where they recorded yet another triumph over the champions in a 1-0 victory thanks to a rare goal from Danny Malloy.

Sept 4th 1954, Brockville Park

Falkirk 4 - 0 Dundee

And so it was against this backdrop that my Dad and I travelled by, first, bus to Alloa, and then the train to Falkirk, to see if Dundee could keep up the good work in the League.

"Falkirk's a bit of a bogey team at Brockville," Dad said to me in caution as we walked up to the stadium, almost as if to prepare me for the worst. He was right. We lost 4-0. I honestly have no recollection of the game except walking pretty sorrowfully to the bus station with my Dad for the trip home. I think my subconscious must have wiped out the memory to save me from too much pain!

Heartbroken, I got off the train from Falkirk at Alloa, where we then had to walk to the bus station. It was a Wednesday evening and we had to wait for about half an hour for a bus to come along to take us home. It was a cold night and as we waited, as if to make matters worse, it started to rain.

"We must be daft," my Dad said jokingly. That was the first time I had heard my Dad say those words, and in the years to come, they were to be echoed many times over as we followed the fortunes of "Bonnie Dundee"!

In February, Dundee were drawn against Rangers in the Scottish Cup, and despite drawing the first game at Ibrox in front of 58,000, before an afternoon crowd of 26,000 at Dens, Dundee lost the replay 1-0, thanks to a Tommy Gallacher own goal.

In the next eight games, Dundee's inconsistent side was evident; three wins, three draws, and two defeats. With only a single fixture left to play, Dundee sat in eighth spot in the table. But for young Caproni, this was to be the highlight of the season.

The venue: Brockville Park, Falkirk. The occasion: the last game of the season. The Dark Blues, regardless of the result, would finish comfortably in mid table. Falkirk were sitting five points behind and safe from relegation to Division Two (Motherwell and Stirling Albion had been relegated). So the result, in reality, mattered not a jot as neither side would likely move up or down the league, irrespective of the outcome. But I wanted to go out on a high. So to me, it was a matter of life or death!

April 30th 1955, Brockville Park
Falkirk 2 - 2 Dundee

The weather was gloriously sunny for that time of year and Dad and I had set out early by, again, first the bus to Alloa and then by train to Falkirk. As we approached the ground, the local pipe band could be heard from within the stadium and, once through the turnstiles, I nervously climbed the steep steps to take my place in the stand. My tummy was churning with excitement.

What a wonderful era that was in Scottish football, a healthy crowd of 12,000 was testimony to that. What provincial clubs would give nowadays to get such a crowd for a meaningless last game of the season!

This was the first time that I had - in the flesh - seen Dundee actually wear dark blue, as in the previous two games I had seen them play that season they had worn their change strip of white shirts and blue pants. It was good to see my team in their true colours as most of the newspaper cuttings that I kept showed the team in their traditional famous dark blue jerseys.

Dad and I seemed to be the only Dundee supporters there as we appeared to be surrounded by Falkirk fans. In these days there was no segregation - which could be quite daunting!

The game started and Falkirk went ahead 1-0, and then, early in the second half, they then made it 2-0. However, just as the words, “We must be daft,” nearly rolled off my tongue, fearing we would never score, that great Dundee servant, Albert Henderson, pulled one back to make it 2-1. There was some hope! The game then started to peter out and some Falkirk fans around us had already started making their way to the exits. I anxiously asked Dad, “How long to go?”

“It’s about time up son,” he replied.

“C’mon Dundee!” I yelled at the top of my voice, unwilling to believe that this was how the last game of the season would end. Then, as if he heard my shout, George Christie, Dundee’s left winger, cut in from the wing and let fly with a screamer of a shot that flew into the Falkirk net for the equaliser! I jumped onto my feet, shouting with sheer joy, my dark blue and white scarf raised high above my head in triumph! Then the whistle sounded for full time. It was a 2-2 draw but it seemed like a victory for me! Dundee? They were the best team in the world!

Chapter 3

"But Dundee Played The Football"

Season 1955-56 started with a real disappointment for me. Dad had said that he would take me to Airdrie for the opening game of the season, but by lunchtime on that day, the rain was so heavy that there had to be a doubt about the game going ahead, and as we would have to have travelled by train and bus, we decided not to go. I remember standing upstairs in my bedroom looking out of the window praying for the rain to go off - but it didn't. But, God, in a way, was good to me - we lost 4-0!

October 8th 1955, East End Park

Dunfermline Athletic 2 - 1 Dundee

The next Dundee game that I remember seeing was at Dunfermline. Another "bogey" team, Dad had said! Just how many "bogey" teams did Dundee have?? There was Falkirk, Dunfermline, and then it was later learned to be Clyde as well! And so this "bogey" theory was proven, with Dunfermline winning 2-1; a Tommy Gallacher goal not being enough for Dundee to share the points. It was a game from which we deserved to take something; it was so disappointing not to have at least got a draw.

So the train and bus journey home was a sad one for Dad and me. I really thought that I was going to see my team win that day.

October 29th 1955, Brockville Park

Falkirk 0 - 0 Dundee

In the lead up to this latest encounter at Brockville we had whacked Raith Rovers 6-3 away from home, which was a great result, and we got a point at home against Killie. So things seemed on the up.

At Brockville that day, Dundee 'keeper Bill Brown produced one of the best displays of goalkeeping that I would ever see; it was down to his heroics that Dundee managed to get a draw. I recall one particular save that Bill Brown made that day, that had it of been in front of the TV cameras today, the save would have been replayed over and over again. It was simply out of this world. Falkirk's midfielder, Jimmy McIntosh, hammered the ball goal wards from around ten yards but Brown seemed to arch his back and somehow palm the ball over the bar. A truly incredible piece of goalkeeping!

The next time that I would be able to see my team play would be on Christmas Eve. In the seven games played leading up to the match, we won four, lost two and drew one, so it would have been fair to say that I was confident of a victory against Stirling Albion.

Christmas Eve 1955, Annfield Park

Stirling Albion 0 - 0 Dundee

Dundee's game was at Annfield Park, the old home of Stirling Albion. The Albion were firmly entrenched at the foot of the league and it was just a week before that Dundee had trounced St Mirren 5-1, so it was with some optimism that Dad and I travelled by bus to Stirling. However, in following the Dark Blues, as I was to learn many times over, being confident of a win shouldn't ever be part of the Dundee supporter's make up. The game ended 0-0.

That draw was like a defeat to me as I really expected us to win. To be honest, we were actually lucky not to have lost the game. It was thanks to another magnificent performance by Dundee keeper Bill Brown that we didn't. So there was still no win recorded on young Caproni's scorecard.

February 4th 1956, Tannadice, Scottish Cup, 5th Round

Dundee Utd 2 - 2 Dundee

The Scottish Cup was always a welcome relief from the grind of the league but for me there was not the same excitement as there would be today, when the draw heralded a local derby with United at Tannadice. United were in the Second Division at the time and most definitely were the city's "second" team. By then, the Dark Blues had won two of the country's three major trophies while lowly United had never even come close, so there wasn't the same competition or rivalry then.

I wasn't actually able to go to the match but I fully expected a Dundee win. (Oops, what did I say about being confident?) It seemed strange to be talking about "the fifth round" of the Scottish Cup when in reality Dundee hadn't played in any of the previous rounds, but in these days, the bigger clubs seldom played in the earlier rounds.

At that time, of course, there were no up to the minute progress reports and scores from all over the country coming in on a minute by minute basis as there is today. No, in these days, at around 4.45pm, the classified results were announced and we had to wait until all *four* Divisions of the *English* League - and sometimes non-League results as well - *before* the Scottish results came through. Bear in mind also that we had no idea even about the half time scores. So as the Scottish Cup results were being announced there was more than a little trepidation felt when I heard, "Dundee United, 2,"………but almighty relief when, "Dundee, 2," followed!

Obviously I was pretty disappointed that we hadn't won but just glad that we were still in the cup!

The attendance at Tannadice had been 20,000 and on the following Wednesday, even although the game was in the afternoon (as there were still no floodlights at that time), another 17,000 turned out at Dens for the replay. Playing in winter without floodlights was always tricky, especially on a rainy, misty kind of day, and in these days there was no white ball either! And 2.00pm kick offs......ah, the good old days!

It always amazes me that 17,000 turned out on a Wednesday *afternoon*. I mean most of these guys who were at the match would be working - or at least, *should* have been working! Jock Mortimer, a Dundonian who moved to Alloa and a friend of mine and my Dad's (more about Jock later in the book!) was at the match and he indicated that almost all of his mates were at the game as well - apparently they all took a "sicky"! I was stuck at school but my mind was forever wandering to Dens Park, which unfortunately my teacher seemed to notice, as I got quite a few rows for not paying attention to what she was saying!

Anyway, goals from Merchant, Stables and Henderson saw the Dark Blues win 3-0 to go comfortably through to the next round.

United, according to *"Rex"* of the Sunday Mail, had come out with their sleeves rolled up ready for a day's work while the men from Dens put on their top hats and tails and went to town! Dad loved that review. Dundee's football skills and short passing game had been the difference. Class always tells.

February 28th 1956, Dens Park

Scottish Cup, 6th Round

Dundee 0 - 1 Rangers

In the sixth round, we drew Rangers at Dens Park. At ten minutes past four on a Saturday, if you tuned into the *"Home Service"* you would hear the following: "This is the Scottish Home Service Association Football. A commentary on the last half hour of one of today's Scottish Cup matches. Dundee versus Rangers (or whatever was the top game of the day), your commentator is George Davidson." The game at Dens was the selected commentary match and my ear was glued to the radio. But there was to be no happy ending as before a crowd of 42,500, we lost 1-0.

Dad tried to console me by stating that although Rangers had won, Dundee had played the football!! It was a saying that Dad used many times whenever we lost. It wasn't *always* the case but, generally speaking, Dundee were a very good passing side. My schoolmates were having none of it though and gave me continual stick for my football persuasion!

Not Another Bogey!

Soon after that traumatic episode, another visit to Brockville in March gave me no further cause for celebration as "bogey" side Falkirk continued their fine run against us with a 3-1 win. Ian Stables scored our goal and a young centre forward called Alan Cousin made his Dundee debut that day, convincing the watching press that a star was in the making - he would later go onto become a Dens Park legend. (Later that season, the big forward would appear against the mighty Manchester United, Bobby Charlton and all, in a friendly at Dens. He scored in a 5-1 Dundee win. Yes you've read it correctly, **5**-1!)

At the end of the season, we did win a trophy. The Forfarshire Cup! Okay, it wasn't the Scottish Cup but, for me, at least it was still a cup.

In the semi final we defeated Dundee United, again! This time it was a 2-1 win for us at Dens, with Jim Chalmers and Billy Birse being the scorers. In the final at Dens Park, four goals by George Merchant and another two from Ian Stables saw the 'Dee canter to a 6-0 victory over Second Division Montrose.

However, even though I was delighted to win the Forfarshire Cup, overall, the season had been disappointing. A 13th position finish was the worst placing we'd had since Dundee had been promoted in 1947.

Next season would be better - I hoped!

Chapter 4

This Is More Like It!

August 11th 1956, Dens Park

Dundee 1 - 0 Motherwell

Season 1956-57 opened with Motherwell visiting Dens Park, and a goal from George Christie was enough to get Dundee off to an encouraging start.

The Dark Blues had been drawn against Motherwell, Airdrie and Raith Rovers in their League Cup section, and as the games were on a Saturday/Wednesday sequence, six games were played between August 11th and September 1st.

Dundee won their opening four games, a successful run that I had never experienced before! A draw at Raith Rovers tempered the feeling a bit but a 7-1 victory against Airdrie at Broomfield confirmed what, of course, I already knew - that Dundee were the best team in Scotland!

September 12th 1956, Dens Park

League Cup Quarter Final, 1st Leg

Dundee 7 - 3 Dundee United

In the quarter final of the League Cup, we were drawn against the old enemy - United - in a two-leg fixture, the first of which was in front of a crowd of 20,000 at Dens Park. Dundee 7, Dundee United 3 was the score (What would I give for seven goals against United today!)! Outside right, Jim Chalmers, who became a bit of a favourite of mine, had a blinder of a game netting three times, and with Black, Christie and O'Hara netting as well, and of course George Merchant getting his customary goal, United were well beaten.

Although United had done well in the first half, Dundee's fitness and quality had always been in evidence and the Dark Blues were never in danger against their lower league rivals. When the score came through on the radio I jumped up and down, barely being able to contain myself! *Two* seven-goal victories in *two* weeks! Yep, Dundee were THE team alright, and I would let all my school friends know!

We did, however, lose the second leg 2-1 at Tannadice, which rankled just a little. United clearly were up for the game but, with the Dark Blues four ahead on aggregate, Dundee did just enough to steer themselves into the next round. It was a moral win for United but there was no doubting Dundee's superiority over the two games.

The good form continued with a 4-2 win over Aberdeen in front of 20,000 at Dens. However, we suffered a 2-1 reverse against Hearts at Tynecastle on September 29th. It was our first defeat of the season but, still, that didn't dampen my enthusiasm as I waited on "the big one" - the semi final of the League Cup.

October 6th 1956, Ibrox Stadium, League Cup, Semi Final
Partick Thistle 0 - 0 Dundee

We had been drawn against Partick Thistle and the game was to be played at Ibrox. The match was on a Wednesday evening and so, at school, the lead up to the match was all that occupied my mind, much to the consternation of my teacher! Later, the result seemed to take ages to filter through. "Partick Thistle nil," - my heart was pounding - "Dundee......nil." Nil??? I really expected to hear that Dundee had won. Still, at least we hadn't lost.

So it was now down to the replay. Partick, it seemed to me anyway, were getting all the praise in the National Press in the Central Belt and it annoyed me, even at that young age, that there seemed to be a West of Scotland bias and that Dundee just seemed to be ignored. All that though just made me more desperate for a win. However, early in the first half of the replay, Dundee found themselves down

2-0. Goals from Christie and O'Hara however levelled the score and Dundee pressed for a winner. But Thistle, against the run of play, scored a third with a free kick. With about twenty minutes left, Dundee piled on the pressure but the "Jags" just held on enough to win. My Dad heard the score on the radio and, as I was up in my bedroom, he shouted the score up to me. Heartbroken, I took my football out in the back garden and played the game all over again in my head. We definitely won that time!

It would be December before I would see my team in action again and, once more, it would be at Brockville Park. "Why did Falkirk have to be Dundee's bogey team?" I mused, as my Dad and I travelled through to the game. Still, maybe this would be the day that Dundee would "burst the bogey". In the six matches that lead up to the Brockville match we had only lost once, winning four times and drawing one. Included in one of the victories was a 2-1 win over Celtic at Dens, so we were on a decent run and, dare I say it, I was confident. Oh dear, when would I ever learn?!

December 1st 1956, Brockville Park

Falkirk 1 - 1 Dundee

Unknown to me, my Dad had arranged a special surprise for me. He had written to Dundee goalkeeper, Bill Brown, who was a bit of hero of mine, and had arranged for me to meet him after the game. Bill Brown had a great game that day, breaking the hearts of the

Falkirk players and fans alike with a series of wonderful saves; and a last minute goal from George O'Hara gave Dundee a share of the points! Falkirk had dominated and Dundee had Brown to thank on many occasions but having said that, O'Hara's last minute goal was a cracker and I was up on my feet cheering that one, I can tell you! Later, I was in awe, when after the game I was introduced to Bill Brown. It had been a memorable day - but still, no win.

Feb 2nd 1957, Dens Park, Scottish Cup, Fifth Round

Dundee 0 - 0 Clyde

Enter Clyde - yet another of Dundee's "bogey" teams! Clyde were in the Second Division at the time but sweeping all before them in their quest for promotion. In fact, they went through the whole league campaign with only one defeat: 4-1 away to Forfar. And although on paper it was First Division against Second, Clyde were so far ahead in the Second Division, that their promotion to the top tier was more or less assured. Dad cautioned that not only were Clyde used to winning, they were of course another of those confounded "bogey" sides so I was a bit apprehensive about the outcome.

I always hated listening to the scores coming through whenever Dundee's score was announced first, for if the announcer stated, "Dundee nil," most times what followed was not good news. On this occasion, well, it wasn't exactly good news but I suppose it could have been worse: 0-0. According to *Sports Report,* Dundee had completely dominated the game but, in front of 22,000 fans, were denied what seemed to be a perfectly good goal by Billy Birse. So they had to be content with a draw and a replay at Shawfield. If only Birse's goal hadn't been disallowed; if it had stood, according to the report, there would have been no way back for Clyde. But such is life when following the Dark Blues! We just never seem to get these breaks, I told myself. There I was, barely turned ten years old and already feeling the strain of being a 'Dee!

The replay was on the following Wednesday afternoon and I remember asking several men on my way home from school if they knew what the score was. To be honest, no one seemed remotely interested but then they wouldn't would they? No one seemed to care about any team outside the Old Firm in this part of the world. I had another mump and moan to myself about the unfairness of it all, before going into the Newsagents. The shopkeeper, who knew that I was a Dundee fan, seemed to take great pleasure in informing me that Clyde had won 2-1. I was not a happy bunny!

Clyde had been leading 2-0 until the Captain, Doug Cowie, pulled one back for Dundee, who had piled on the pressure looking for the equaliser and in a frantic spell had struck the post twice. But the Second Division side held on and we - were out. Now I had to face the wrath of my schoolmates all over again. "I'm going to start supporting Celtic," I said in a moment of disgust to my Dad!

"I've had to put up with that for over thirty years," my Dad replied. "We'll come again. Support Celtic if you want but remember, Dundee's got the class". Talk about indoctrination! By the time I had got to bed that evening I was already thinking about Dundee's next game against Queens Park on the Saturday. I shouldn't have bothered though - we lost 2-0.

Dundee, however, all throughout their history, have been unpredictable; winning and losing when least expected, and it was no different when strong going Partick Thistle came calling to Dens a fortnight later.

The Dark Blues gained some measure of revenge for their semi final defeat by trouncing the Glasgow side 5-1. Dad was right, I thought to myself. Dundee *do* have the class and any thought of switching my allegiance to Celtic was well and truly buried!

March 2nd 1957, East End Park

Dunfermline Athletic 1 - 1 Dundee

According to my "Wee Red Book", which every supporter in these days seemed to have as it provided all the fixtures for the season as well as a host of other information, it would be around four weeks before I would be able to travel to see my team in action again. Dundee had won their last two games and I couldn't wait to see them in action in a visit to Dunfermline on March 2nd. It was, however, another disappointing 1-1 draw with a Billy Birse goal giving us a share of the spoils. Please, God, when am I going to see a win???!!

Typical Unpredictable Dundee

Dundee had had a chequered season. Sometimes looking like genuine challengers then, just as my hopes were rising, they would make sure that I didn't get too cocky and suffer a string of defeats. Then, in typical Dundee fashion, when you were at your lowest ebb, they would unexpectedly win. It was like a rollercoaster of emotions. It was OK when you thought that they would lose and unexpectedly win - that was great. But when you thought that they would win and then lose, it was all too much to take.

In the last two games of the season, after losing four games on the trot, almost as if they were playing with your emotions, again, Dundee finished off the season with a 3-0 victory over fourth placed Raith Rovers. However, despite the encouraging last game performance, Dundee had finished a disappointing tenth in the league. And even though the Dark Blues had reached the League Cup semi-final, they had seen their Scottish Cup hopes flounder in the Fifth Round against Second Division Clyde. There was no Forfarshire Cup victory this season either as they lost 5-2 to Brechin - at Dens!

"Is supporting other teams as frustrating?" I asked myself.

Chapter 5

A Win At Last!

On reflection, at the beginning of season 1957-58, it was quite difficult to believe that the team that would bring the Championship to Dens in around four to five years time, was starting to take shape.

Bobby Cox, Alex Hamilton, Alan Cousin and Hugh Robertson all featured regularly in a campaign that could be described as, at best, brilliant and, at worst, downright awful. Overall, they were pretty inconsistent.

Season 1957-58 saw the Dark Blues lose six and five goals respectively to Hearts, another five to Third Lanark, seven to Airdrie, four to Raith Rovers and four to Queen of the South. Amazingly, however, Dundee themselves scored five against Queens Park at Dens and seven at Hampden, five against Celtic and five against Partick Thistle. You just didn't know what to expect!

February 15th 1958, Starks Park

Scottish Cup, 2nd Round

Raith Rovers 0 - 1 Dundee

When the Scottish Cup draw was made it didn't look as if the "gods" had looked kindly on Dundee. We were drawn away to strong going Raith Rovers at Kirkcaldy. One of my fondest memories had been when Dundee had played the Rovers at Kirkcaldy the previous season and had, against all the odds, won 2-1. Rovers, who finished fourth that season, had beaten Rangers 5-1 the week before but true to form, the 'Dee came up trumps when least expected!

This term though, Rovers had turned us over at Dens 2-0 and just six weeks earlier we had been trounced 4-0 at Starks Park. However, as we had learned in seasons gone by, the cup can be "funny". Dad and I, accompanied by my uncle Bill (originally a Rangers man but he converted from the light blue to the dark!!), made our way to Kirkcaldy, more in hope than in expectation, for the second round of the Scottish Cup. Getting to Kirkcaldy was a long and tediousome journey; travelling, again, by bus from Tillicoultry to Alloa, where we then had to walk about 500 yards to the train station to catch a train to Dunfermline. There, we had to change for Kirkcaldy and then hike a fair old distance to Starks Park.

The queues to get in were long but we managed to get a good seat in the stand, and when Dundee took the field, I gave it all I had.

"Dundee for the Cup!" I shouted at the top of my voice. As both teams were required to change if there was a colour clash, Raith, who also played in dark blue, lined up in red shirts with white pants and Dundee wore their change strip of white shirts and blue shorts.

The crowd of approaching 13,000 had hardly settled in their places, when Dundee scored. George Christie, who normally played on the left wing, was this time playing on the right. He sent over a dangerous ball, which Alan Cousin swept home - right footed, from around 15 yards! This wasn't in the normal script! I was on my feet whirling my scarf around. "C'mon Dundee, give us another one!" I shouted. We made it to half time with it still being 1-0, although there were distinct warning signs that the second half was going to be stressful!

In the second half, it was one-way traffic towards the Dundee goal and Bill Brown put on one of the best displays of goalkeeping (again!) that anyone would likely ever see. The big agile Dundee keeper saved everything that Rovers could throw at him and, believe me, there was plenty for him to do. High and low crosses, shots, diving at the feet of forwards, he did it all. The game was in danger of boiling over however, with tackles flying in fast and furious and, mid way through the second half, Dundee's Albert Henderson and Jimmy McEwen of Raith were sent off after a full-blown fisticuffs session ended in referee, Syme, having to physically intervene. Apparently Henderson and McEwan were buddies off the park but you would never have guessed it!

Bill Brown continued to break the hearts of the Raith players and fans alike. Then, late in the second half, the guy in front of me, who had been urging Raith to inflict some damage on the Dundee goalkeeper, snapped, and shouted, “Kick that bloody keeper!” That was enough for my uncle to retaliate by lifting the cap from the guy’s head and pulling it right over his eyes whilst at the same time telling him to “shut up” or, ahem, words to that effect! It could have sparked a nasty incident but the Rovers supporter, I think, took one look at my uncle who was as tough a guy as you could ever meet and decided that he’d better indeed just shut up!

Several minutes later, which seemed like an eternity, the final whistle blew. 1-0! We had won……at last! I was on my feet cheering wildly, much to the disgust of the Rovers faithful around me. The journey back home, this time, passed far too quickly. Oh, it’s great when you win! (The week previously we had won 1-0 at Tannadice in a Forfarshire Cup match against United. Two away wins on the trot - things were on the up!)

March 1st 1958, Dens Park, Scottish Cup, 3rd Round

Dundee 1 - 3 Aberdeen

I eagerly awaited the draw for the next round: Dundee versus Aberdeen. Not too bad, I thought, we could win this. The week before the game however, we lost 4-0 at Queen of the South though and my confidence began to evaporate a little.

My Dad, my uncle and I, all made the trip to Dens, so this meant an early start; the bus to Stirling, the train to Dundee and then another bus up to Dens. The queues for the stand at Dens were lengthy and, just as it was our turn to pass through the turnstiles, a notice went up: "Stand Full". Aghh! This meant an almighty rush for the enclosure. We jostled for position in a long, almost never ending queue. We then heard the roar of the crowd for the teams running out and I was beginning to get really concerned that we weren't going to get in at all! When we did eventually get in I had to wriggle my way to the front so that I could see, with Dad and my Uncle standing a few rows behind. Thankfully, it was just in time to see the teams kick off. However, this huge policeman then came and stood right in my view and, despite less than polite requests from people around me, he didn't move. So I decided to squeeze along past several more seemingly huge adults in order to see the pitch. The omens off the pitch weren't good and it turned out to be that way on the pitch as well.

My memory of the game is one of Dundee dominating completely - but being caught on the break. Aberdeen lead 2-0 and although a Hugh Robertson goal gave us hope, a late Dons' goal, ironically scored by Bobby Wishart, who would go on to star in our Championship win, sealed our fate. We lost 3-1 in front of 28,000. This time, it was a long, tiresome and not very enjoyable trip home. We could have - *should* have - won that game.

The League Of Extraordinary Gentlemen

For the first time, Dundee's league position was starting to give us some concern as we seemed too close for comfort to a relegation spot. After the defeat to Aberdeen in the Cup, we won 2-0 against Third Lanark but then dropped three points out of the next four available. Suddenly, a game against Queens Park at Hampden was taking on more significance than we would have liked. Queens were well adrift at the foot of the league but there was only five points separating ourselves and second bottom East Fife. It seemed to me that the West of Scotland press loved it. The jolly old Queens could put Dundee right in trouble!

A Win At Last!

March 22nd 1958, Hampden Park

Queens Park 2 - 7 Dundee

With Dad working until one o'clock, getting to the match at Hampden would have been impossible, so that Saturday Dad and I instead went to Recreation Park to watch Alloa. In these days there was a half time scoreboard - no loudspeaker announcement of the half time results, and if you didn't have a programme, which identified the letters corresponding to the various games, it was quite difficult to find out the result you wanted. However, according to the half-time board, Dundee were winning 5-2 at half time. Wait, 5-2?? That can't be right, we thought.

Later, however, as we were walking to the bus station we bought the early addition of the evening newspaper. Half time: Queens Park 2 Dundee 5. It had been right enough! Further down the column were some full time results: Queens Park 2 Dundee 7. *Seven*???!!! Were we happy!!

Then, at Dens the following Saturday, in dreadful conditions, we whacked in five against third placed Celtic to win 5-3. So it was with this newly found assurance that we travelled to Falkirk with a bit of belief to see if Dundee could make it three wins in a row.

April 12th 1958, Brockville Park

Falkirk 0 - 2 Dundee

Season 1957-58 was drawing to a close and the team were showing signs that their recent goal scoring form had given them credence and conviction. In this game, they never looked like losing, although to be fair, typically, they waited until the closing minutes before scoring the second and clinching goal. Probably just to keep with tradition and keep all their fans nerves on the edge!!

Dad and I had a great view of that second goal. We seemed to be right behind the ball as Alan Cousin appeared to "toe poke" the ball into the far corner of the net. It had been the first time that I had seen Dundee win against the "Bairns", with two goals from Alan Cousin giving Dundee the deserved victory!

What an extraordinary team Dundee were. I honestly don't believe that they themselves knew which Dundee was going to turn up on any particular day. On a good day they were capable of beating the best, but on a bad day, well, enough said!

Then, as season 1957-58 drew to a close, there was even further encouragement for me. In Dundee's last game, against Rangers, another Alan Cousin goal gave Dundee victory at Ibrox! Although I wasn't at the game, I watched it with much delight on the television at night. What a great way to end the season!

My euphoria of seeing my team triumph at Ibrox helped cloud the fact that they finished in eleventh place. This pegging did nothing much to excite the faithful for the coming season. But for me, at least I had seen my team in the flesh win - twice!! Next season couldn't arrive quickly enough.

Chapter 6

A Mixed Bag

Season 1958-59 would turn out to be a really mixed bag, inspiring the chequered emotions that seemed to be part and parcel of being a Dundee fan.

My family and I were returning from a holiday in Whitley Bay and, approaching Edinburgh, the bus stopped to allow people to go to the toilet, or whatever they fancied doing with the half hour or so when the bus would be parked, before embarking on the last lap home to Clackmannanshire.

It was after five o'clock on a Saturday evening and, as there was no radio on the bus, I sought out a newsagent to find out the score from Dens Park in the very first game of the season; a League Cup tie against Partick Thistle. Finding a shop quickly, I bought the early addition of the *Evening News* and scanned down the column of results in the "Stop Press" section. Dundee 2 Partick Thistle 1. Yes! A victory! I gave my Dad the thumbs up from outside the bus. However my joy was to be short lived as after getting back on the bus, Dad noticed that I had been looking at the half time results. A quick scan further down the page revealed the full time scores: we had lost 3-2. My holiday feeling quickly dissipated! Was I sick! "Scunnered," was the word that my Mum used!

August 20th 1958, Brockville Park

Falkirk 2 - 5 Dundee

The first league game of the season was at Brockville Park, Falkirk - never a very happy hunting ground for Dundee in recent years. We had, however, won there the previous season, the first time that I had seen a victory in my numerous visits to Falkirk.

In the lead up to the game, we had played two away fixtures in the League Cup campaign, winning 2-1 at Motherwell, which was an excellent result as the Lanarkshire side would go on to finish third in the league in the coming season. But typical of Dundee, they then lost 1-0 at Palmerston against Queen of the South who were relegated that season.

At Brockville Park, Falkirk, on the following Saturday, it was gloriously sunny as Dad and I took our seats in a crowd of 13,000 who had turned up to welcome the teams out. Falkirk were in their changed strip of tangerine shirts and white pants and Dundee wore their traditional dark blue. This was to be the day that a Dundee side, oozing with class, were to well and truly "burst the bogey".

Alan Cousin notched a hat-trick and Ally Hill and Davie Curlett added to Falkirk's misery in a resounding 5-2 victory. Actually, Dundee were brilliant that day. Over the years, good Dundee sides had struggled at the tight confines of Falkirk's Brockville Park but the Dark Blues' refined football was just too much for "the bairns" that day. 5-2 was actually being kind to them - we could have scored quite a few times more! There were signs that this Dundee side were beginning to show the "class" that my Dad had always said Dundee sides had!

Another Bag Of Allsorts

Dundee's mixed form continued however and they won only one out of their six League Cup fixtures but then found themselves joint top of the league when Aberdeen were beaten 2-1 at Dens. They then suffered a 4-1 trouncing at Starks Park against Raith Rovers but bounced back with a 1-0 victory against strong going Kilmarnock at Dens. It is an understatement to say that we never knew what to expect from the boys in Dark Blue!

September 27th 1958, Ibrox Stadium

Rangers 1 - 2 Dundee

It was against this setting that Dundee travelled to Glasgow to play league leaders Rangers. Rangers were, as you would expect, the big favourites but a classy Dundee performance with goals from Alan

Cousin and an own goal from Willie Telfer saw the men from Dens claim their second consecutive win at Ibrox with a 2-1 win. The game was on *Scotsport* in the evening but, as we only had BBC, my Dad and I walked to my uncle's house at the other end of Tillicoultry to enjoy watching the 'Dee turn over the 'Gers!

Although school was never something I looked forward to, I couldn't wait for Monday morning to come so that I could "sock it" to my Rangers supporting schoolmates! However, I would pay for that later on in the season!! Clearly I wasn't learning quickly enough that when you're Dundee fan you can't afford to be smug.

October 11th 1958, Dens Park

Dundee 3 - 3 Hearts

The first time I ever saw a league match at Dens was when my Dad took me to see Dundee host Champions Hearts, in season 1958-59. The Tynecastle side had won the title the season before by 13 points, scoring a massive 132 goals in 34 matches. It was sure to be an exciting match, and with Dundee losing only one of their opening five league games, an 18,000 crowd rolled up to Dens to see, arguably, the two best footballing teams in the land. One of Dad's colleagues at work had a car and he had arranged with Dad to drive us to Dens. It made a happy change from roughing it on buses and trains to get to Dundee, that's for sure.

Dundee were in their change strip of white shirts and blue shorts with Hearts in their traditional maroon. After only ten minutes or so, I was up on my feet cheering vehemently, as Alan Cousin put us ahead. However, ex-Clyde centre forward, Ally Hill, who had been forming a good partnership with Alan Cousin, seemed to injure himself in the build up to the goal and spent the rest of the half limping on the right wing. With no substitutes in these days, Dundee were effectively playing with ten men and Hearts took full advantage, scoring three times before half time to lead 3-1 - I worried that we were going to get a real hammering.

In the second half though, despite Hill still limping and nothing more than a nuisance value on the right wing, Dundee rallied and, urged on by the big home crowd, pulled one back from the spot! The first time I ever saw Dundee get a penalty! Doug Cowie calmly side footed the ball into the net and it was game on at 2-3. What a magnificent player Doug Cowie was. This was a player who could pass the ball equally well with both feet, tackle, head the ball - he just had everything. In today's multi-million pound world of football, he would have been sought after by the very best and would have finished his playing days a very rich man.

Despite effectively being a man short, the white shirted Dark Blues pressed for an equaliser. Finally, late on in the game, a magnificent volley from Alan Cousin put Dundee back on level terms. 3-3! The ball was crossed from the left wing and big "Cous" hit it on the drop from around sixteen yards, flying passed the Heart's keeper without him knowing much about it! What excitement! I shall never ever forget the feeling I had when the equalising goal went in. What a game!

The car journey home was a very comfortable and happy change. Out of the jaws of defeat! Dundee are THE team, I thought!

December 13th 1958, East End Park

Dunfermline 2 - 1 Dundee

In the ten games that led up to this match, Dundee in typical unpredictable and chequered fashion had won four, drawn four but encouragingly had lost only twice. And the week before we had beaten "in form" Hibs 2-1 - so I was pretty confident that we could get a result at East End Park! Agh! I said that word: confident. Why did I have to be feeling that way?? The outcome was almost inevitable.

A Davie Sneddon goal wasn't enough to give us a share of the points in a 2-1 defeat. I really thought that we would win that day but, although we seemed to have a lot of the ball, to be honest, we never really looked like saving the game. The Dark Blues, though, were hovering around the top four or five in the league and many were saying that it was the best Dundee side since the George

Anderson days. Even the Glasgow Press were saying that this could be Dundee's year for the Scottish Cup!

January 31st 1959, Balmoor Stadium

Scottish Cup, 1st Round

Fraserburgh 1 - 0 Dundee

When the draw was made for the cup, I thought we couldn't have got an easier draw. However, my enthusiasm was somewhat tempered a little when Dad reminded me of the Berwick Rangers game, when we lost 3-0 to the "C" Division side!

Along with Hearts and Motherwell, the Dark Blues were being described as one of the best footballing sides in the country and, although our form had dipped, losing the last three League matches, surely a non-league team couldn't put us out of the cup? Could they? Yes, they could. Fraserburgh 1, Dundee 0. My world came crashing around me. I had been glued to the TV screen for ages waiting for the result to come through. Then the dreaded teleprinter told its tale of woe. I looked. I looked again. Oh no, I thought, this just cannot be true! I looked for the third time hoping that I had been mistaken. Nope. It was 1-0 alright - and we were out.

Dundee had dominated the game which, given the difference in status, was what was expected of a top League side. But the Dark

Blues scorned chance after chance to go ahead, and when Fraserburgh scored right on the half time whistle it should have been a wake up call for the Taysiders. I even remember the name of the scorer for Fraserburgh; a guy called Hugh Strachan - the very mention of his name still haunts me! In the second half it had been a bit like the "alamo" as Fraserburgh had "battoned down the hatches " and defended as if their lives depended on it. Try as we might, we just could not breach the Highlanders' defence and we were out.

Suddenly, school on Monday was something to be feared and, believe me, I took some stick for the failings of my beloved Dark Blues! It is difficult to believe that the team which lost at Fraserburgh that day had players in it's ranks like Bill Brown, Doug Cowie, Jimmy Gabriel, and four players who would help bring the Championship to Dens only three seasons hence; Alex Hamilton, Bobby Cox, Alan Cousin and Hugh Robertson. It just didn't make sense.

Credible But Not *In*credible

After the Dunfermline game on December 13th and the Fraserburgh debacle had *almost* been forgotten, it would be March before I would see my favourites again, against Stirling Albion. In the four games leading up to the match against the Albion, we had lost twice, won 2-1 against Clyde and had got a pretty credible 1-1 draw against Celtic at Celtic Park.

March 7th 1959, Annfield Park

Stirling Albion 0 - 1 Dundee

Excited to see the Dark Blues in the flesh again, I can remember standing at the hospital end of the ground (for anybody who remembers the geography of the old Stirling Albion stadium), behind the goal that Dundee were attacking, hoping to see a goal - and I did! I had the perfect view of Alan Cousin's goal; the net bulged as the master of the double shuffle hammered the ball home! The Albion had been having a decent season and sat just below the middle of the league (which was probably their best ever campaign in the top division) and teams going to Anfield in that season found out that it was no easy task. Having watched the Albion a few times, I knew that Dundee would have a hard game on their hands and so I was delighted to come away with full points from what was always going to be a tricky fixture. The Dark Blues triumphed 1-0!

On the bus home to Tillicoultry, only a few miles from Stirling, I was the only person sporting Dundee colours - but I enjoyed that. Wearing the team colours is always good when you've won!

Although we finished the season in a credible fourth spot, nine points behind Champions Rangers, my satisfaction was dulled a bit with the transfer of Davie Sneddon - an industrious and classy inside left - to Preston North End for £12,000. But even worse was to follow. My hero, Bill Brown, was transferred to Spurs for £16,500 - a record fee at the time for a goalkeeper.

Fourth spot was okay but I harboured hopes of a title challenge next season. However, even at the tender age of twelve, I had learned enough about being a Dundee supporter to realise that to become over ambitious could lead to another Fraserburgh experience. Better, I thought, to just wait and see!

Chapter 7

More Of The Same

August 8th 1959, Fir Park

Motherwell 4 - 2 Dundee

The opening League Cup game of season 1959-60 was at Fir Park and, despite being 2-0 in front, the Dark Blues eventually went down 4-2. The game was on the radio and we joined the commentary when Dundee were 2-0 up and, unfortunately, I then had to listen to the four Motherwell goals going in with more than a degree of frustration!

Living in Tillicoultry, with Dad working until 1.00pm most weekends, and still not having a car, it was impossible to get to Dens so we used to go to see our local senior clubs; Stirling Albion one week and Alloa the next. For midweek games there was even less chance of us seeing the Dark Blues unless their game was perhaps at Falkirk or Dunfermline.

On the following Wednesday after the defeat at Motherwell, Dundee were hosting Hibs at Dens Park. I would loved to have gone but it just wasn't possible so we made our way to Annfield Park, Stirling, instead, to watch the Albion take on Kilmarnock - even though my heart was definitely at Dens.

Later, the half time results came through: 2-0 to Hibs. My head dropped into my hands. Dad then lifted my spirits, as always, countering my pessimism with the comment, "Dundee will score three in the second half!!" I smiled, excited at the prospect, the ever eternal optimist! But deep down, I truly doubted the wisdom of his words.

Making our way to the bus station after the game, I rushed to buy an evening paper and quickly scanned the "Stop Press" where all the full time results were recorded but they were not in alphabetical order - not even by division! There were results from the English Fourth Division mixed in with results from our own leagues. It was like trying to find a needle in a haystack! But then I eventually saw the result I was looking for and couldn't believe my eyes: Dundee 4 Hibs 3!! A win! I punched the air in delight! Goals from Cousin (2), Robertson and a rare goal from Doug Cowie had seen Dundee fight back to win in front of over 17,000 at Dens. Dad was right! Okay, he was one out but was he psychic or something??

Or perhaps it was just the years of experience in being a Dundee fan that lead to him realise that with Dundee, anything can happen!

A League Of Their Own

Dundee's League campaign started with a 3-0 win at Aberdeen with goals from Cousin, Waddell and Hill, sealing an emphatic Dundee win. However, two defeats and three draws in their next five games saw Dundee slump to the bottom half of the table - but not for long. Five wins in a row saw them climb the league table and a 5-0 win at Firhill against Partick Thistle had even the West of Scotland press tipping them for a title challenge. But, yes, you guessed it, in typical Dundee fashion they quickly poured cold water over any enthusiasm that was generated, losing to Hibs 4-2 and then 2-1 to Airdrie at home.

This was typical Dundee, I thought. One minute you think that they are the best team in Scotland and the next you can't believe how appalling they are. "Son, I've lived my life like that," Dad confessed. "They'll come again though," he added optimistically.

Well, with the words barely out of my Dad's mouth, what do you know? They visit Celtic Park and come away with full points. Bonthrone, Robertson and Henderson being the goal scorers in a 3-2 win! Nobody had given them much hope for Parkhead, so that made it all the sweeter. It was always such a great surprise when they unexpectedly won!

Good Local Produce

Dundee were now getting a reputation of producing great home grown talent, although keeping the talent at Dens proved to be difficult at times. Bob Shankly, who had by this time succeeded as manager to the departed Willie Thornton, later recorded his dissatisfaction when Dundee lost yet another of their star players to England with the hugely rated Jimmy Gabriel transferring to Everton for £30,000. It was unfortunate that a player of Gabriel's potential was sold before he was anywhere near his prime. The Dundee fans had had to endure the departures of stars like Bill Brown, Danny Malloy and Davie Sneddon in recent years, and now Gabriel. Just when would this end, we thought.

But thankfully there appeared to be a conveyor belt of young talent coming through at Dens Park. Alan Cousin and Hugh Robertson were already established in the first team and there were even more knocking on the first team door, most notably, Andy Penman and Ian Ure. And just waiting in the wings, soon to burst onto the scene, was a tall lanky inside left called Alan Gilzean.

Championship success and European glory was just round the corner for many of the players and there is no doubt in my mind that Bob Shankly - with the signings of Wishart, Seith and Smith - masterminded the finishing touches to what was to be a wonderful side. Willie Thornton however, despite his stewardship being less rewarding, should perhaps get some credit for bringing some of the most talented youngsters in Scotland to Dens Park.

December 12th 1959, Annfield Park

Stirling Albion 0 - 1 Dundee

The following Saturday after the Celtic match, I was able to see Dundee in action as their fixture was at Annfield Park, Stirling.

Despite their lowly league position, the Albion gave the Dark Blues a real tough game, just as the season before, but an Alan Cousin goal gave Dundee the win and full points. Phew!

Happy New Year! - Or Is It?

Now, I'm certain that most Dundee fans and indeed any football fan will recognise the feelings that I am talking about when I say that New Year's Day was absolutely ruined if, as used to happen when the games were actually played on January 1st, you lost your festive day fixture. Many a festive period was ruined in the Caproni household if we suffered defeat! However, this New Year's Day was not something to mourn.

January 1st 1960, Dens Park

Dundee 4 - 1 Aberdeen

Going into the match against the Dons, we had won three out of the last four games and so I was confident that we would win. Worry not that I used that cursed word, confident, as this time it was justified! We gave the Dons a bit of a drubbing with goals from Henderson (2) Robertson and a young Andy Penman. Happy New Year, everybody!!

A healthy 16,000 crowd had rolled up to Dens for the North East derby and they watched a Dundee side in rampant form. At no time during the match did the Dark Blues ever look like losing. According to the *Scottish Home Service* radio report, we could have won by more and sixteen year old Andy Penman was the name on every one's lips after the youngster had capped an excellent performance with a well taken goal.

According to my "Wee Red Book", the next time that I would be able to see my team was at Dunfermline. In the lead up to the match at East End Park we only recorded three wins out of ten and, before a crowd of 30,000 at Easter Road, we went out of the

Scottish Cup by 3-0 to Hibernian. A complete contrast to New Year's Day.

March 12th 1960, East End Park

Dunfermline 2 - 2 Dundee

Dad and I made our way to East End Park via Bus and train and a long walk to the stadium and witnessed a cracker of a match! Dunfermline were battling against relegation and led twice, but we showed some fighting spirit and came back with a vengeance with goals from Alan Cousin and an emerging Bobby Waddell, giving Dundee a share of the points in a 2-2 draw. In the end, however, I felt that we should have won it.

Our title hopes had realistically vanished around February and, although Dundee managed a 0-0 draw at Ibrox, a 1-1 draw against Arbroath and 1-0 defeat at Ayr saw them slip too far behind. After these two games however, the team started to find their form again, albeit too late to challenge for any silverware. Partick Thistle were dumped 3-0 at Dens then the Dark Blues gained some form of revenge over cup foes Hibs. The Easter Road side were sent packing with a 6-3 thumping with Andy Penman notching a hat trick.

April 23rd 1960, Dens Park

Dundee 4 - 1 Stirling Albion

The last home game of the season saw Dundee host Stirling Albion and as we lived only twelve miles from Stirling, Dad, perhaps cheekily, paid for seats on the Stirling Albion supporters bus for the trip to Dens. There I was, with my dark blue and white scarf carefully hidden in my pocket as I boarded the bus. It was strange to listen to the comments of the opposing supporters on the way up to the match. It was a vital game for the Albion because a defeat would see them relegated. The general consensus of opinion seemed to be that Albion hadn't much of a chance against what the Albion supporters were describing as, "One of the best teams in Scotland". I couldn't have agreed more!

We finally got to Dens and, sheepishly, Dad and I descended the steps from the bus at Dens Park (little did I realise that I myself would later go on to play for the Albion!). That day, we saw a devastating performance from a young Alan Gilzean who notched a hat-trick, with Alan Cousin scoring the other goal in a 4-1 win. Amazingly, nine players on show that day would be in the squad that would bring the title to Dens in the not too distant future!

Going home on the bus, with my scarf again concealed, it is an understatement to say that it was difficult to contain my joy! However, I have to say that I felt just a little sorry that the Albion had been relegated as I always had a soft spot for them. But such is life!

Although Dundee finished on the same points as Rangers, and ten behind second placed Kilmarnock, they were twelve behind Champions Hearts and had to settle for fourth on goal average - but this was third equal as far I was concerned!

Alan Cousin finished the season as top scorer with 17 goals to his credit. And, we *again* claimed the Forfarshire Cup with two goals from Andy Penman and another from Albert Henderson being enough to see off Forfar Athletic 3-2!

Easy! Easy! Aren't Dundee fans so easily pleased?!

Chapter 8

Champs In Waiting

Up until they got promotion, I never really disliked Dundee United, in fact, it was on the contrary as I used to look for their result in the Second Division. When they visited Recreation Park to play Alloa in their promotion year, I stood with their supporters wearing my dark blue and white scarf, which was almost the same as their own black and white colours at the time, not cheering them on as such but not wishing they would be beaten - like I would be today!!

But then an extremely heart racing episode happened. "Hey!" my pal shouted to the United fans, "This guy supports your biggest rivals!" It was like the cat had been let loose amongst the pigeons. Some United fans darted their attention to my scarf and realised that it was in fact navy blue and not black and white! It was time for a quick exit!

Up until that point I had never really thought about United as being our greatest rivals. Aberdeen really took that mantle and the "North

East Derby" fell into the same fixture category at New Year, when traditionally all the local derbies were played, such as Rangers versus Celtic and Hearts versus Hibs. So when United got promotion, it was no big deal for me and I guess that most other Dundee fans, like me, probably saw United as easy meat for the coming season.

Field Of Dreams

Away from the rigours of following Dundee, I was playing regularly for my school team and had been selected for Clackmannan County Schools, under fourteens. I was then spotted by a Dundee scout, who arranged three days training for me - at Dens Park! My dream was to be a professional footballer and, more specifically, to play for Dundee! It was almost surreal that there I was, aged 13, actually playing on the same Dens Park pitch along with guys like Alan Gilzean and Ian Ure, etc., during a training stint. I had to pinch myself several times just to make sure that it was real! After the three days were over, Bob Shankly asked if I had enjoyed it and then said that, as I was only thirteen, they would be keeping an eye on me, checking my progress. This was good enough for me - Bob Shankly actually saying to me that the club would be checking my progress! Wow!

The dream scenario continued and season 1960-61 started with a bang with three victories in a row in the League Cup campaign: 5-0 against Raith Rovers, 2-1 away to Ayr United and, before a crowd of more than 18,000 at Dens, a 4-1 victory over Aberdeen. I was floating!

August 24th 1960, Starks Park

Raith Rovers 2 - 1 Dundee

The opening fixture of the League Campaign was against Raith Rovers at Kirkcaldy and, in light of our great start to the season, Dad and I decided to make the long wearisome journey to Kirkcaldy on a Wednesday evening to see if the Dark Blues could keep up their good form. This is where the dream feeling ended and the nightmare began.

It was a terrible night, weather wise, with the rain just teeming down. It was an awful night football wise too; we lost 2-1. Alan Cousin scored Dundee's goal but the team never played to the form that they had shown in the opening games. Trust us to pick this game. "We must be daft," Dad mused as we made the long, tiresome journey home.

Typically though, Dundee visited Starks Park again three days later on the Saturday, in the League Cup, and an Alan Gilzean hat-trick brought a 3-0 win. Dad and I weren't at that match. Typical. But that's life when following the fortunes of the Dark Blues.

Dundee's League Cup campaign was going tremendously well however, winning all six games culminating in a 6-0 drubbing of Aberdeen at Dens, with Gilzean notching a hat-trick! I was actually getting on the train from Stirling to Alloa with a pal after we had been to see Stirling Albion play when I heard someone who was looking at a newspaper shout to his mate, who obviously was an Aberdeen fan, 'The "Dons" got hammered 6-0 from Dundee!' Nice one!

The following week, in the first game of the League Campaign at Dens, "Gillie" did it again with another three goals against the Dons but on this occasion, Dundee had to be content with a 3-3 draw.

The Dark Blues were then drawn against Rangers in the League Cup quarter final. When I heard the draw had paired us with Rangers, I was disappointed we hadn't been matched with "lesser" opposition. I thought a smaller team would have given us more of a chance of progressing, but Dad was quick to point out that Dundee seemed to be better when everybody was writing them off. Hmm, I thought, there might be something in that! In the first leg at Ibrox the team had played well but unfortunately lost 1-0, but I wasn't disheartened. Dundee were unbeaten at Dens Park up until that point and I was optimistic that we could turn things around in the return fixture, in front of our own supporters.

In the second leg at Dens, Gilzean uncharacteristically missed a penalty and then two further goals from Rangers saw Dundee fall 3-0 behind on aggregate - but the game wasn't over yet. An amazing fight back with two goals from Cousin and one from Penman saw Dundee go ahead which meant they were equal on aggregate. However, there was to be no happy ending. Two late goals from Rangers saw the Ibrox side - rather luckily I have to add - progress to the semi final.

A crowd of 33,000 watched the game and, although Dundee lost, they had proved that they were capable of competing at the highest level. From a personal point of view, I thought that at last, I was going to see a sustained challenge from the men from Dens Park.

A New Enemy!

Sandwiched in between the Rangers games, was the first local derby in the First Division between Dundee and United at Tannadice since season 1925-26. Over 20,000 crammed into the ground to witness this historical game. I desperately wanted to be there too but, with my Dad still working 'til 1pm on Saturdays and still not having a car, getting to Dundee for matches was still always so difficult. So I had to be content to listen in to the radio or TV for the result. By this time, *Grandstand* had introduced the teleprinter, which gave results of games just as they finished. I'm sure the kids today must laugh at all the "stone age" technology!

It was great when Dundee were away from home and the opposition score came up first and read, "nil". Phew! The pressure was then off. The worst result after hearing that could only be a draw. However, if it started with the home team 3, which it did that day, my heart always sunk - and this time, quite rightly so. United had won 3-1.

I honestly couldn't believe it. I had always looked on United as a Second Division team and definitely the poor relations in the City of Dundee. Suddenly, all feelings of goodwill to our near neighbours vanished. From then on, the Tannadice team were enemy number one!

' Dee Bounce Back!

The results over the next few weeks however, were great; five wins in a row took Dundee to the top of the league. One of these wins was against Rangers at Ibrox where, before a crowd of 43,000, Alan Cousin scored the only goal of the game. Even school was a pleasure after that result and I wasted no time in letting my schoolmates know that it was the *Dark* Blues and not the Light Blues that were the big team in Scotland!

But there I was, bragging again! When, oh when, would I ever learn that supporting Dundee is really meant to be a humbling experience?

October 29th 1960, East End Park
Dunfermline 4 - 2 Dundee
Five wins in a row and top of the league (top of the league!), we travelled with great expectation to East End Park. Yep, the league leaders were facing Dunfermline and, yes, you have probably guessed, with our confidence high, we lost. And our smugness was to be punished even more; Dundee won only *two* of their next eleven fixtures and, by January, had slipped down to mid table.

January 7th 1961, Dens Park
Dundee 3 - 0 Dundee United (!!)
The eagerly awaited return derby with neighbours United came around (oh, I so - how can I politely put it? - disliked them now!) and I was ready to show them who was boss! - and, so it seemed, were Dundee.

The temperature had dropped considerably that day and there was a doubt about some of the fixtures going ahead. But despite the imperfect conditions, which on numerous occasions had tended to favour the City's underdogs, Dundee were dominant.

Away from the tight confines of Tannadice, a classy Dundee exploited the wide-open spaces of Dens Park and in front of a crowd of 22,000, Bobby Wishart - recently signed from Aberdeen - scored twice, with Bobby Adamson notching a third to send the Tannadice men away empty handed! When the score came through on the teleprinter, I jumped up and down like a yo-yo!! Then, later, *Sports Report* stated, "Dundee could have won by more." One team in Dundee, there's only one team in Dundee!!!

Oh So Victorious! - But Not For Long

Later that season, on a Wednesday evening in February, goals from Wishart, Cousin and a brace from Gilzean saw Dundee dump Rangers 4-2 and thus do the double over the Ibrox side! But on the following Saturday, Dundee were due to play the "Gers" again, this time though, in the Scottish Cup. The Dens men had been a bit of a thorn in the side of the Ibrox club and there were signs that the Dark Blues kind of fancied their chances of a double success over Rangers, all within a week. My confidence that Dundee could triumph waned a little however, when I heard that Doug Cowie had picked up an injury in the mid week match and wouldn't play. This meant that the defence had to be reshuffled with Ian Ure, who had been outstanding in the Wednesday fixture, moving to wing half and Billy Smith coming in at centre half, with young Alex Stuart deputising for Doug Cowie. Still, I thought, we could win this!

February 11th 1961, Dens Park

Scottish Cup, 2nd Round

Dundee 1 - 5 Rangers

We decided to go the game and we took the early train from Stirling to avoid the Rangers fans travelling through to Tayside. It was the strangest of games. Rangers, with a strong wind at their back, seemed to score every time they were up the pitch and led 4-0 at *half time*. Cousin reduced the deficit in the second half but, despite Dundee's domination, the Ibrox side broke away to score *again,* making it 5-1. In front of a 32,000 crowd, Dundee's defence, so sure against Rangers in the previous game, seemed at sixes and sevens. Before they had settled, the wind assisted Ibrox side had basically wrapped up the game before half time. Dundee seemed to have the lion's share of the game but Rangers were the masters at putting the ball in the net.

It was another long and depressing journey home, this time though, to make matters worse, we were surrounded by singing Rangers fans on the train to Stirling which, I can assure you, was not pleasant. I sure was glad to get off. And then I had school to face too. I had given all my mates “stick” after the 4-2 victory on Wednesday, but now I was going to pay for that!!

Jock Mortimer had been at the game also and, when I met him the following week, he kept saying that Rangers had been lucky. Although it seemed strange to say that, especially when the margin of the win had been so emphatic, in a funny way, I knew what he meant. For long spells we had never been out of the Ranger’s penalty area but just couldn’t get the ball in the net, and then Rangers would break away and score.

My Dad first met Jock when he was in his twenties. In those days (1930’s) most local works had their own football team and Dad played for Harlands, a large engineering factory where he worked as a turner, long before he went into the insurance business. Dad was a goalkeeper and a pretty good one at that, according to men I’ve spoken to who saw him in action.

Jock played for the Railway and, after a game against Harlands, he overheard Dad singing the praises of Dundee in the dressing room after the game. Jock then shouted over, “Aye, Dundee’s the best team in Scotland!” It was very unusual to hear anyone with a Dundee accent in Alloa and certainly anyone in that area praising Dundee, so a friendship blossomed from the mutual love for the Dark Blues and they remained chums ever since that day.

Jock was the most fervent Dundee fan that I have ever known. He was absolutely biased towards everything Dundee and I only once heard him criticise a Dundee player. Jock was in awe of any Dundee team member and I recall, when I had a spell helping with the Dundee reserve side, I took him into Dens and out on to the pitch; it was like watching somebody who had just won the lottery!

Reserve A Seat For Us!

A couple of weeks later Dundee hosted Dunfermline at Dens in a League game, but of course because Dad worked until 1pm, and still without transport, getting to Dens was impossible, *but* we were able to travel to Dunfermline to see the reserves who were playing at East End Park!

The reserve league was great in these days and most teams had a mixture of experienced players who were "getting on a bit" and up and coming younger players. In the main, it was generally good football that was on offer. I can't remember much about the match except that I remember thinking that Ronnie Crichton, our right winger, was not a bad player *and* being surprised at the size of the crowd, which would have been in the region of about a couple of thousand. Anyway - we lost 5-0!

Nowadays, we would have known the score at the first team game at Dens before we had even left East End Park but, in these days, communication was hardly swift and so, waiting at the train station, Dad decided to ask a railway porter if he knew the score at Dens. Thinking we were Dunfermline fans the porter shook his head and replied. "We got a real doing today at Dens - 4-1 for Dundee!!" Ya beauty!!!

April 22nd 1961, Dens Park

Dundee 2 - 2 Motherwell

In the second last game of the season, Dundee were due to play Motherwell at Dens and in the games leading up to the match our chequered form continued with three wins, three defeats and a draw. I had written to Andy Penman (who, a couple of seasons later, would be one of Dundee's title winners and would go on to become a legend at Dens Park) as he was a right winger, the same position as I played, and although I was equally as comfortable on the left I had modelled much of my game on his. So I thought that meeting him would be inspiring and a thrill for me - and it was! He replied with a nice letter AND two tickets for the game!

Dad suggested that, as he would not be able to manage, maybe I should go up to Dens with my pal, Maurice, (who was a Hibs supporter) on this occasion. I did, and it was a great adventure for us; travelling by train to Dundee on our own and, of course, meeting

Andy Penman in the player's entrance - and then getting into the Stand for free!

For an end of the season affair, the game was really entertaining, considering there was nothing really at stake in the match. A 2-2 draw was probably about right with Bobby Waddell and Hugh Robertson scoring for Dundee.

A Chequered Past

In a season that was chequered to say the least, in the final game of the League campaign at Tynecastle, we suffered a 2-1 defeat to Hearts. To be honest, I always liked winning the last game of the season as it kept me going over the close season, so to speak, and so I was disheartened when I heard that we had lost.

However, the spell in mid season that took the team to the top of the league had been exciting and there were some great performances on which to look back. A 6-0 win over Aberdeen, a 3-0 win against United and a double over Rangers.

Dad and I thought that if we could just find a wee bit of consistency, then maybe, just maybe, next season could be our year. We would wait and see.

Chapter 9

We Are The Champions!

Season 1961-62 lives on in the memory of every Dundee supporter who was fortunate enough to witness it. When the whistle went to signal full time at Muirton Park, Perth, 28th April 1962, over 20,000 Dundee fans celebrated the winning of the greatest prize of all - the Scottish League Championship!

I am not ashamed to say that I danced on the turf that afternoon, along with thousands of the other ecstatic fans and, to this day, I can still hear my Dad saying that he had waited over forty years for that moment.

If anyone, at the beginning of the Championship winning season, and especially after the opening League Cup tie against Airdrie at Dundee, had forecast the scenes at Muirton Park, then they probably would have been laughed out of Dens Park.

The Start Of A Great Adventure

August 12th 1961, Dens Park, Scottish League Cup

Dundee 2 - 0 Airdrie

The Dark Blues had been drawn with Airdrie, Rangers, and the now defunct Third Lanark, in their League Cup section. Over 13,000 turned out for the opening game of the season against Airdrie, including my Dad, Jock, his son, James and, of course, me. It was a glorious August afternoon. We stood at the Provost Road end, almost at the corner flag, and it wasn't long before all the Dundee fans were on their feet as a Bobby Wishart rocket from 20 yards screamed into the Airdrie net! What a view we had of it too! Then, an Alan Cousin goal in the second half gave Dundee full points.

It wasn't a particularly good game however, despite the result, Dundee were not at their best. Personally, I didn't think that it had been too bad but clearly I was in the minority as most supporters were worried for the future. When we made our way to the exits we heard a battle hardened "old timer" say, "It's going to be a long dreary season!"

August 23rd 1961, Brockville Park

Falkirk 1 - 3 Dundee

In the League Cup, away games against Rangers and Third Lanark followed but were lost 4-2 and 3-2 respectively. In the League

Campaign, Dundee were scheduled to kick off at Falkirk and although the Brockville side had been, on several occasions, a thorn in the side of the Dark Blues, in more recent times Dundee seemed to have the measure of the "Bairns", as they were nicknamed.

Dad and I, along with Jock and James, arranged to meet at Alloa train station on the Wednesday evening so that we could again travel together to the match, this time at Brockville. We called ourselves the Clackmannanshire Branch of the Dundee Supporter's Club!

That night it really hit home more than ever that the consequence of being a Dundee supporter meant experiencing extreme highs, intense lows and everything else in between - and sometimes all within a very short time span! With Dundee 3-1 ahead and less than thirty seconds left, Jock turned to me and said, "Do you think we can relax now?" to which I replied, "Surely even we can't lose two goals in thirty seconds?!"

"I've seen it happen!" was Jock's reply!

I actually now realise what he meant! I remember well a Dryburgh cup match against Celtic at Dens. We were leading 1-0 and the referee was looking at his watch; the clock was registering well over the ninety minutes. Then suddenly, Tam Gemmell played a slack pass-back to our goalkeeper, Thomson Allan, and a Celtic player nipped it in to net the equaliser. The match went to extra time and we lost 2-1. I also remember being 3-0 up on Morton at Dens on one occasion and finished up drawing 3-3!

Going back to the game at Brockville, the remaining seconds could not tick by quick enough, and the hell was only added to by Jock's comments of us having a habit of losing goals in the last minutes of games gone by. Then: The final whistle blew! Relief! My nerves settled a bit. We had won!

That evening though, we got an inkling of what the season would bring, with quality strikes from Wishart and Cousin - but little did we know that this was the start of a magical and great adventure!

What's The Story? More Glory!

Dundee's good form continued with a 5-0 League Cup win over Airdrie, an exciting 1-1 draw with Rangers at Dens, and in the final game of the section, goals from Cousin and Penman gave us a share of the points at Cathkin, against Third Lanark.

September 9th 1961, Dens Park

Dundee 4 - 1 Dundee United

Next up was the eagerly awaited first derby of the season against United and a 20,000 strong crowd turned up to see Dundee outclass their near neighbours with a scintillating performance. The Dark Blues really turned on the style.

On the left, Robertson torpedoed his way down the wing whilst on the other side, Smith, chipped, flicked and caused all sorts of bother to an over run United defence. Penman, Cousin and Gilzean interchanged with bewildering speed and United just had no answer. Dundee were absolute quality, oozing class. In the end, it was goals from Penman, Robertson, an own goal from Briggs and a magnificent volley from Gordon Smith that gave the Dens Parkers full points in a 4-1 win. Smith's was the pick of the goals; with the veteran winger taking a cross from the left on the drop from around sixteen yards and hammering an unstoppable shot high into the net.

The highlights were on Saturday night *Scotsport* and, although it was nearly always the Old Firm that featured, it would be the first of many times that season that Dundee would feature on the Saturday evening programme. That Saturday evening seemed to take an age to pass until it was time for the match to be shown but when it did come round, I savoured every moment! Unfortunately, there were no video recorders in those days so I couldn't tape it, which was probably just as well; I would have spent hours watching the game over and over again, probably to the detriment of my schoolwork!

The following two matches brought mixed fortunes: a 3-1 reverse at Aberdeen was followed by a 2-0 victory over Hearts at Dens. Gordon Smith, at thirty-seven, was again the inspiration for Dundee against the Tynecastle side. Although Gilzean scored the two goals, it was the veteran Smith on the right wing who caused panic in the Heart's defence. On the other wing, Hugh Robertson continued his fine form also, and the little winger's trickery and perfect cross found the head of Gilzean, who had no difficulty heading home Dundee's second goal.

However, it was at Cathkin Park, home of Third Lanark, which would prove the start of an amazing unbeaten run.

September 30th 1961, Cathkin Park

Third Lanark 1 - 3 Dundee

We couldn't get to the match at Cathkin but with the Glasgow press waxing lyrical about two of Ranger's young players, John Greig and Willie Henderson, we decided to go and see the Ranger's reserves, who were the visitors to Stirling Albion's Annfield Park, in a reserve league fixture. Rangers won 6-0 but the match at Cathkin was where our hearts were, and at the bus station on our way home we learned, from the early edition of the *Evening Times*, that Dundee had won 3-1! Cathkin was never an easy place to go and Third Lanark were a really decent side but, despite being under a bit of pressure, the Dark Blues had weathered the storm so to speak and, in the end, had seemingly cruised through the match with Gilzean (2) and Cousin registering on the score sheet.

That result brought Dundee level with Rangers and Kilmarnock at the top of the league! We had seen it all before of course but we started to believe that, this time, just maybe, we were on to something. Then, with barely that thought entering our heads, before 14,000 at Dens, joint leaders Kilmarnock were beaten 5-3 in an eight goal thriller with an Andy Penman hat-trick being the highlight of a very good Dundee performance indeed.

October 14th 1961, Fir Park

Motherwell 2 - 4 Dundee

It wasn't until the following week, however, against Motherwell at Fir Park, that the West Coast Press sat up and took notice. Motherwell were always a bit like ourselves in as much as they were always praised for their good football but seemed to lack the killer touch. Games between Dundee and Motherwell were for the purists and were always entertaining - and this game would turn out to be no different.

Dundee had got off to a great start when Penman scored from the spot in the first minute. Motherwell then equalised twenty-five minutes later but only four minutes after that, Alan Cousin restored Dundee's lead, cutely slipping the ball into the net from a long throw by Bobby Seith.

Motherwell fought back in the second half however and drew level after seventy minutes. But Dundee just seemed to raise the tempo even further and Smith restored their lead with a brilliant header from a Cousin cross. Then, with thirteen minutes left, Gilzean scored Dundee's fourth and clinching goal!

It had been a real classic of a match and Dundee's performance had been outstanding. Even the West of Scotland press were beginning to believe that this was no "flash in the pan". Jack Harkness of the *Sunday Post* wrote, "On this showing, Dundee has everything that Championship stuff is made of. Method and skill. Coolness in tight corners. The happy knack of switching quickly from innocent outfield play to devastating danger in the goal area." This result meant that Dundee led the league for the first time!

Is This Real Or Am I Dreaming?

So it was to Dunfermline the following week that the Clackmannanshire Branch of the Dundee Supporters Club travelled, "bhoyed" that their team was in pole position at the top of the First Division!

October 21st 1961, East End Park

Dunfermline Athletic 1 - 2 Dundee

As has been recorded earlier in this book, Dunfermline was never a very happy hunting ground for the Dark Blues. On this occasion, Dundee started with their usual line up but early in the first half an injury to Gordon Smith upset the rhythm of the side. It was then no real surprise when strong going Dunfermline (who would finish fourth that season) went ahead before half time.

In the second half though, despite Smith being no more than a passenger on the right wing, Dundee forced the pace and, urged on by a large following, equalised through a fantastic goal from Alan Cousin. Cox started the move with a pass to Wishart who found Penman with a controlled pass and Andy sent Cousin on his way. Alan was wide on the right when he received the ball and he took it to almost the bye-line before - from an almost impossible angle - firing it past Connachan in the Dunfermline goal.

Then, eight minutes from time, the big centre forward caused pandemonium in the large contingent of Dundee fans behind the goal when he notched the winner. A free kick from Cox went soaring towards the far post and Cousin rose above everybody to head for goal. Connachan, in the Dunfermline goal, appeared to think that the ball was going wide but it suddenly appeared to swerve and went into the net off the far post. 2-1 Dundee! This roused Dunfermline to a big final effort but goalkeeper Liney was brilliant during the closing stages and Dundee held on to win.

These were the type of games that prospective Champions had to win. That day, it was another happy journey home for the small, but triumphant, Clackmannanshire Supporters Club!

School for me, finally, was great! After enduring years of taunting by Old Firm fans for my football persuasion, I finally could jeer back at them. I must have been unbearable! But it was official - we were at the top of the league, so we must be the best team in Scotland! There was no argument!!

However, despite all that rejoicing, the uneasiness of being a Dundee supporter never left us. At around 4.45 pm every Saturday, Dad and I must have lost pounds in nervous energy as we waited on the Dundee results! One such game was against Partick Thistle at Dens when a crowd of over 16,000 saw Dundee leave it *very* late before an Alan Cousin goal secured a 3-2 win, which kept them at the top of the table. However, it was the next two weeks that finally convinced the watching (and listening!) public and the Glasgow press that Ranger's champions' status was under threat.

On The Attack!

Celtic and Rangers were the next two matches on our fixture list, with Celtic being the first in the firing line.

November 4th 1961, Dens Park

Dundee 2 - 1 Celtic

Almost 25,000 rolled up and witnessed a classic contest. Celtic pushed the Dens Parkers hard but it was the Dark Blues who went ahead in the eighth minute. A Robertson corner was headed out and Wishart let fly with a right foot shot that soared past a helpless Frank Haffey in Celtic's goal. Celtic equalised before half time and in the second half they put the Dark Blues under considerable pressure but, in the fifty-ninth minute, Dundee broke away to score. Andy Penman raced down the left wing and his cross, at first appearing too heavy, went to Cousin who chased and controlled the ball away out on the right before looking up and crossing for Gilzean to net the winner!

November 11th 1961, Ibrox Stadium

Rangers 1 - 5 Dundee

And so next on our hit list was "the big one". Rangers versus Dundee at Ibrox. Dundee went into the match three ahead of second place Killie and five ahead of Rangers, who were in third place, although the Ibrox side had two games in hand.

I, myself, was beginning to make a name on the football front and had been selected to play for Clackmannan County Schools against Perthshire at Muirton Park on the Saturday morning, which meant I couldn't attend the Dundee game. Unfortunately, however, my team took a bit of a drubbing and lost 4-1.

On the bus back from Perth, the main subject under discussion was the impending game at Ibrox and the general consensus of opinion was that Rangers would "sort us out". Just wait and see, I thought.

So with Dad working and me playing, that day, Jock Mortimer made his way on his own to Ibrox but was turned back at Glasgow Buchannan Street Station by police who had been drafted in to advise Dundee fans travelling to the game that the match was off due to foggy weather. Jock, disappointed, travelled back to Stirling and took in a junior game at Dunipace instead. However, this is where he learned that in fact the Dundee match had not been postponed at all and, furthermore, the result at half-time was 0-0! Amazingly, the fog had lifted just before kickoff.

At this time, a half time score service had been initiated on the *Grandstand* programme and, watching anxiously at home, Dad and I were reasonably happy with the 0-0 score line. We both felt that a draw would be a good result for us. Bear in mind also that there was no up to the minute goal alerts or anything like that in these days, so at around quarter to five we were both glued to the screen, adrenalin running, as the newly introduced *Grandstand Teleprinter* service recorded the results of games just finished. Every time the printer started our hearts leapt! Still no result. And then it happened: Rangers 1 - Dad and I both held onto each other - Dundee....5!! Pandemonium in the Caproni living room! 5-1! We couldn't believe it! Later, poor Jock Mortimer said that he didn't know whether to laugh or cry when he heard the result!

The game was on television in the evening and was amazing to watch! Rangers had the better of a tense first half but the second half had hardly got underway when Gilzean headed home after a splendid move. And before the Ibrox players and fans alike had recovered, he did it again - less than two minutes later! The Dark Blues were in control and broke from defence with lightning speed, and it was no surprise when "Gillie" scored a third with around fifteen minutes left. One Sunday newspaper reported that, at one stage, Dundee seemed to be, "Toying with their opponents." And although Rangers pulled one back with five minutes to go, Gilzean hammered in a wonderful fourth; Gordon Smith, oozing class, weaved this way and that until he found Robertson who flicked forward for Gilzean to rocket his shot passed a helpless Ritchie in Ranger's goal. Andy Penman then rubbed salt into the considerable Ibrox wounds with a fifth - right on full time! What a game!

The crowd, because of the rumours that the game was postponed, was still a credible 38,000 plus but it would have been comfortably, I reckon, over 60,000 had normal circumstances prevailed. Countless supporters buses from Tayside had been turned back due to the stadium being enshrouded with the dense fog.

However, the result was something to behold. Now school was getting even better! I never, ever thought I could have said that, as I was no scholar! As it happened, my class had been asked to do a project on football and everyone had to choose a team in the First Division. I chose Dundee, of course, and then we had to produce a graph plotting the progress of that particular team. Never did I ever look as forward to a lesson as I did at that time!!

Things Are Still On The Up!

November 18th 1961, Dens Park

Dundee 5 - 4 Raith Rovers

It was the following Saturday, when Raith Rovers came calling to Dens, that Bob Shankly stated that he felt that he had a side that could indeed win the championship. In these days, Raith Rovers were nobody's pushover and, the week before, they had beaten second placed Kilmarnock 3 -2.

However, things were going according to plan with the Dark Blues, leading 2-1 at half time. Soon though, somehow, the league leaders found themselves 4-2 down with less than half an hour to go. But the big 15,000 plus home support then started to lend a hand, roaring the team on. They were soon rewarded when a dream shot from Wishart, and then, with only four minutes left, a fabulous strike from Bobby Seith, saw the 'Dee back on level terms. With the crowd on their feet cheering Seith's equaliser, only a minute later Dens Park went absolutely wild when Gordon Smith hit home the winner. Dundee had always been known for their classy football but now they had added fighting spirit along with a bit of steel to their play. It was this side of their game that finally convinced Shankly that his team were definitely Championship winning material.

November 25th 1961, Easter Road

Hibs 1 - 3 Dundee

The following Saturday, Dundee played Hibs and so Dad and I made the long journey to Easter Road. The rain was belting down and, although the only cover was in the stand, over 16,000 fans (many from Dundee) braved the elements. In fact, it was the biggest support that I had ever seen at an away game. As there was no segregation in these days, Dad and I seemed to be surrounded by Hibs fans and there was one particular guy who never stopped referring to Dundee as "phoney league leaders". However, with a minute to go until half time, a Gordon Smith cross found Gilzean and the big Dundee marksman rose majestically at the far post to head the ball passed a fully stretched Hibs goalkeeper, much to the delight of the huge Dundee following! I can remember Dad and me on our feet shouting, "It's easy for the league leaders!" That was just what was needed to shut our "friend" up! 1-0 at half time.

Andy Penman then added a second in the next half and, although Hibs pulled one back, a late goal by ex-Hibs favourite Gordon Smith settled the issue. 3-1 for the 'Dee! We were on our way!

It was, unfortunately, becoming increasingly difficult for me to see my favourites in action though because, as well as playing for my school team on Saturday mornings, I was playing for Alloa Y.M. on Saturday afternoons too! Two games in one day!! The afternoon game always kicked off around 2.00pm, which if the game was at home, sometimes gave me time to get home and listen in for the full time results, at least that was something.

A week later, after defeating Hibs 3-1, I was confident of another victory against foot of the league Stirling Albion at Dens. Surprisingly, however, Albion held us to a 2-2 draw - yes even that quality a side could still drop you in it! But any notion that a chink in Dundee's armour was about to show was dispelled the week after when Airdrie were on the end of a 5-1 thrashing at Dens. Then a draw at St Mirren was followed by a 2-1 win over Falkirk. It was an icy Dens pitch on the day of the latter game and Alan Gilzean, to try and gain better balance, wore sandshoes instead of football boots! I couldn't ever really see players of today doing that! But it must have worked as the big Dundee No. 10 scored both Dundee's goals!

On A Roll!

January 13th 1962, Tynecastle Park

Hearts 0 - 2 Dundee

With the inclement weather causing several games to be postponed, Dundee were without a competitive fixture for a couple of weeks. However, any thoughts that rustiness may have set in vanished when they travelled to play Hearts at Tynecastle where, in front of 25,000, Dundee turned in a magnificent performance.

In the first half, Dundee sprayed the ball about in a display that was a joy to behold. With the first time lob, the cheeky flick and impertinent nod, all in the middle of pouncing opponents, they stamped themselves as the sweetest moving football machine in the business. Dundee went ahead in fifteen minutes when Robertson stabbed the ball into Penman, who found Smith on the right with a peach of a pass, and Smith's cross for Cousin was perfection with Alan never having to even break stride as he headed the ball home. Hearts came back into the game but goalkeeper Liney was equal to the task. The Dundonians looked actually to be strolling about.

In thirty-three minutes, Dundee scored a second. Smith flicked the ball to Penman who lobbed to Cousin at the far post. Big Alan rose above all to head nonchantly into the path of Gilzean about eight yards out. But there was no hasty shot. As the Heart's goalkeeper Marshall leapt out, Gilzean tamed the ball instantly, side stepped the 'keeper and almost disdainfully tapped it over the line. It was the ultimate in serviette soccer! "*Rex*" of the Sunday Mail quoted, "Dundee has the Champion's armour. The team just oozes poise and never do they stop playing football".

The crowds were rolling back to Dens and 2-1 victories over Aberdeen and Third Lanark were watched by 16,000 and 17,500 respectively, with another healthy derby crowd of over 16,000 seeing St Johnstone beaten 2-1.

Cup And Out

Dundee fever was everywhere, it seemed. There was even talk of Dundee doing the double, so when the Scottish Cup tie with St Mirren came round, I was more than a little excited!

Almost 23,000 attended for the visit of the "Buddies". My game kicked off earlier than usual and so I had time to take in a local game; Stirling's cup tie against Partick Thistle at Annfield, along with Dad. Our hearts were at Dens though. But major disappointment fell upon us when we learned Dundee were 1-0 down at half time. At the end of the match I made my usual dash to get the early edition of the evening paper. No change - we had lost 1-0. What? *Lost*??? That feeling wasn't as common as it had been in previous seasons. No double for Dundee, I couldn't believe it. Still, I optimistically thought, we were still eight points clear at the top of the league.

February 3rd 1962, Rugby Park

Kilmarnock 1 - 1 Dundee

The following week we visited Kilmarnock and a last minute and hotly disputed Alan Cousin goal gave us a share of the points. With Kilmarnock a goal ahead and the game nearing to an end, the crowd at Rugby Park were making their way to the exits when, in the dying seconds, Seith found Cousin out on the right. Big Alan controlled the ball and hoisted it to the far post. Killie's 'keeper Sandy McLaughlan got both hands to the ball but the referee, to consternation in the Kilmarnock ranks, adjudged that the ball had crossed the line and we went home with a point. Phew! That was a close one. The next four games however, were a disaster.

A Rocky Road

February 10th 1962, Dens Park

Dundee 1 - 3 Motherwell

At Dens, in front of over 19,000, we lost 3-1 to a very good Motherwell team. Worryingly, there were signs that we were going off the boil. Listening in for the result was torture and even worse when we learned the result. That was the first disaster.

February 24th 1962, Firhill

Partick Thistle 3 - 0 Dundee

With my game being postponed, we travelled to Glasgow to Firhill for the match against Partick Thistle. It is the done thing nowadays for teams to be out on the pitch warming up a good half hour or more before the match but back in the sixties it was unusual in the extreme if a team appeared before five to three. Really, to be honest, going into a game without any sort of warm up was, on reflection, ludicrous. When I played, I cannot recall coming out any earlier than five to three and our warm-up consisted of a little run about and a shot in at the goalkeeper! Strangely, though, I cannot recall the same amount of injuries to players then that there is today!

On this occasion, however, Partick Thistle were already out warming up when we took our place on the terracing behind the goal - a good half hour before the kick off. As the game kicked off, Dundee looked a shadow of the side that we had seen in previous games and went on to suffer their biggest defeat of the season, going down 3-0. We were absolutely terrible and that result was being kind to us. A top form Dundee would have cantered to victory but we were really awful that day. "We must be daft," my Dad muttered as we left the stadium. Thoughts of us finishing as Champions were evaporating fast; I was getting those sinking feelings again. And it was to get worse.

March 3rd 1962, Celtic Park

Celtic 2 - 1 Dundee

Next up was Celtic, but despite going ahead from a Bobby Wishart goal, Celtic fought back to win 2-1. That day, Bobby Lennox (who would go on to win a European Cup winners medal) made his debut for Celtic and scored the winner. That was disaster number three.

March 7th 1962, Dens Park

Dundee 1 - 2 Dunfermline Athletic

Then, the fourth disaster. It was a Wednesday evening and I was like a cat on hot bricks waiting for the result from Dens in the rearranged match against Dunfermline. There was no mention of the result on the main news so we tuned into the radio late in the evening and were disappointed (understatement!) to learn that, in front of a crowd approaching 18,000, we had lost 2-1. Just what the hell was going on?

March 14th 1962, Dens Park

Dundee 0 - 0 Rangers

The change in Dundee's fortunes meant that they had now been overtaken by Rangers and so the Dark Blues trailed the Ibrox men by three points. This meant that the game against Rangers was rapidly taking on the mantle of a title decider. Normally, we had never any chance of making it to Dens on a Wednesday evening but a friend of Dad's, who had a leaning towards the 'Dee, offered to run us to the game. I was really excited about the prospect of seeing this game and all day long I could think of nothing else until it was time to leave. "You'll likely get beat tonight," Mum said as we left. "Cheers Mum," I thought!

The atmosphere was electric at Dens as the kick off approached and the crowd of around 35,000 was Dundee's largest of the season. Disappointingly though, Gilzean was unfit and couldn't play and there was a lot of scrappy play as both sides seemed determined not to lose. Rangers lost their centre half, Doug Baillie, to injury in the first half and, although the big Ibrox defender remained on the pitch, he played out on the wing and was really only of nuisance factor. Dundee, sensing an opportunity, went for the jugular but despite being the better side, they couldn't get the vital goal, which would have given them both points.

Back On Track

Confidence, however, began to return with wins over Raith Rovers at Starks Park (3-2) and Hibs at Dens (1-0). After the Hibs game it was learned that United had done us a favour by recording a rare 1-0 win over Rangers at Ibrox. Thanks boys!!

Then, a fighting 3-2 victory over Stirling Albion meant that we were now only one point behind Rangers and it was definitely "game on" again. Dad was at the match at Stirling whilst I was playing somewhere in Glasgow. I heard the score on the bus radio coming home and couldn't wait to celebrate with my Dad.

Next was a 2-1 win over Airdrie, which meant that now, the Derby game against United, on Spring Holiday Monday, would take on even more significance than normal. Derby games were always significant, even if there was nothing at stake, but for Dundee, this match was almost life or death. It was a game in which they could just not afford to drop any points. Even a draw would not be a good result. It was win or bust!

April 9th 1962, Tannadice Park

Dundee United 1 - 2 Dundee

Tannadice was bursting at the seams with 20,000 fans and it was one of the few all ticket league games that I can remember in that era - and it turned out to be a real thriller!

United opened the scoring early on but Gilzean equalised, just on half time. In the second half, mounting Dundee pressure eventually paid off when "Gillie" crashed home a magnificent twenty-five yarder, five minutes from time - the winning goal!

The result meant that we were on equal points with Rangers, who had dropped a point in their own derby with Celtic. "Up wi' the bonnets!" my Dad proclaimed.

Down To The Wire

In the final two games, Rangers had Aberdeen away on the Wednesday evening and a last game of the season at Ibrox against fifth placed Kilmarnock. Dundee had St Mirren as visitors at Dens on the Wednesday and they would finish with a trip to play St Johnstone at Muirton Park. The Ibrox side though, still held the advantage with better goal average.

April 25th 1962, Dens Park

Dundee 2 - 0 St. Mirren

On the Wednesday evening for the visit of St. Mirren, over 20,000 fans turned out to witness what was to be a dramatic night of football. St. Mirren were fighting for their First Division lives so, albeit for vastly different reasons, the Paisley side needed the points just as much as Dundee. Dundee had to respect their opponents though as they had knocked the Dens Parkers out of the Scottish Cup earlier in the season and had gone on to reach the Scottish Cup final, which they had lost to Rangers only the week before. So we had to be cautious.

It was a tricky game to begin with. The Dark Blues, urged on by the big crowd, surged forward but the Saints were dangerous on the break and almost shocked the crowd into silence when they hit the post. But all started going according to plan when Alan Cousin opened the scoring just before half time. The move began when Cox dispossessed St Mirren's Thor Beck and found Gilzean. Quickly, "Gillie" switched the ball to Cousin who then smacked the ball in to the net from eighteen yards. Thunderous cheers all round from the crowd!

News that Rangers were losing 1-0 at Aberdeen filtered through and the excitement amongst the supporters was tremendous. Dundee pushed on for a clinching second goal but then - disaster! With less than 15 minutes to play, St. Mirren were awarded a penalty. The excitement amongst the crowd quickly turned to trepidation. However, although Jim Clunie's shot was a good one, Pat Liney, Dundee's goalkeeper, proved to be the hero of the night with a truly magnificent diving save. Then, less than five minutes later, Andy Penman made it 2-0 and the 20,000 fans roared their approval!

When the final whistle blew, the score from Pittodrie was announced: Aberdeen 1, Rangers 0! The roar that followed could have been heard about two miles away at the harbour!

With Rangers losing at Pittodrie, Dundee were now two points clear at the top of the league. A draw was all that was needed against relegation threatened St. Johnstone on the following Saturday now. This would see them crowned Champions.

Championies, Championies!

Oh Way, Oh Way, Oh Way!

April 28th, 1962, The City of Dundee

In the city of Dundee, Dundee United played hosts to Hearts at Tannadice Park. The attendance was 6,000. But for the majority of the football supporting public in the city, another game appeared to be attracting more attention, more than 10% of the total population of the city, in fact. Over 20,000, travelled the twenty-two miles to the fair city of Perth to see their team, Dundee F.C., the oldest senior club in the city, play St Johnstone.

April 28th 1962, 60 Ochil Street, Tillicoultry

The time was 8.30am. I waved goodbye to my Dad as he left for work. Today, he organised his calls so that he could be back before eleven instead of his usual 1pm. True to his word, Dad was home at the promised time of 11am and, by 11.30, we were both ready. But I had been ready long before then. We waved our goodbyes to my Mum and my sister Margaret and walked down to catch the bus to Alloa, where we met Jock and James at the railway station. With Dundee scarves draped proudly around our necks, James and I waited with our Dads for the train to take us to Perth.

When we reached our destination, we descended excitedly from the train where there were already hundreds of other Dundee supporters. On leaving the station, the Dundee fans burst into song, "Hail, Hail the 'Dee are here!" (Originally sung by the Celtic fans, this was the song that Dundee fans had adopted as their anthem). It made a great noise as it echoed throughout the station!

April 28th 1962, Muirton Park

St Johnstone 0 - 3 Dundee

When we eventually reached Muirton Park, the gates were still closed. It was only ten minutes to two but already there were long queues stretching back around thirty yards as the Dundee supporters arrived in their thousands.

We eventually took our place in the stadium, down at the front right at the corner flag. The ground was full, long before the kick off. The attendance: 26,500. The whole stadium seemed to be taken over by Dundee supporters and I don't recall seeing one single person sporting St. Johnstone colours!

The weather was magnificent and the atmosphere electric. At three o'clock it was almost a relief when the referee blew his whistle to start the match. We were only ninety minutes from glory.

There was an early scare as "Hammy" cleared off the line. St Johnstone, with Alex Ferguson in their line up and Bill Taylor (who was to become a team mate of mine in later years) in goal, fought for their First Division lives in the knowledge that a draw would keep them up.

But with twenty-five minutes gone, after a splendid move and great play from Cousin and Seith, Gordon Smith swung a magnificent cross over from the right wing and Alan Gilzean (who else?!) rose majestically to head it into the net! The huge Dundee support went into a state of delirium! The Dark Blues were now in control and looked a confident side going into the half time break.

In the second half, with around thirty minutes left, a glorious ball from Hamilton found Gilzean and the big striker skipped elegantly passed a Saints defender before sliding the ball into the net for Dundee's second! Then, Andy Penman made certain with a wonderful third goal only a few minutes later! From then on it was a gala day!

The crowd never stopped singing and, as the final whistle approached, hundreds of fans clambered over the barrier at the foot of the terracing. When the whistle sounded, it seemed as if all 20,000 Dundee fans were on the pitch! Dad, Jock, James and I rushed onto the pitch as well! "We want the champs!" was the chant. The Dundee players were carried shoulder high from the pitch and the crowd didn't leave until the players made an appearance in the Muirton Park stand. The dream was finally a reality - we were the champions!!!!

Rangers had drawn their game 1-1 against Kilmarnock, so we had won the championship by three points.

The walk to the railway station was incredible; thousands of fans singing and dancing in the streets. “Bonnie Dundee” echoed from the bagpipes being mercilessly squeezed by a piper in full regalia.

That night, I waited up to see the match again on *Scotsport* and afterwards went to bed with a huge contented smile on my face - and woke in the morning with an even bigger one! I couldn’t wait for Sunday morning to come to read all about it. I must have bought every available Sunday Newspaper possible!

We Did It!

Season 1961-62 had come to an end and I thought back to the comment made by a supporter after the first game of the season, “It’s going to be a long dreary season!” Long, yes, but dreary, it certainly was not!!!! Dundee F.C. were the Champions of Scotland!!

The Dundee league winning team will forever be remembered not just for the fact that they won the League Championship, but for the football style and class that they portrayed as well. The late Bob Crampsey - the renowned football historian - stated on many occasions that, in his informed opinion, that Dundee side were the best footballing side ever produced in Scotland. This was echoed by Arthur Montford, at the time a football commentator of some note, and now a director with Greenock Morton.

Above: Dad and me. Below: "It's going to be a long dreary season!" Bobby Wishart scores against Airdrie in the first game of the season at Dens (61-62)

Airdrie's 'keeper fails to stop WISHART'S shot for Dundee's first goal. COUSIN is the Dundee player in the picture.

Left: "Where did that one go?" Smith nets in a 4-1 drubbing of United at Dens (61-62). Below: Gilzean nets the winner against Celtic at Dens (61-62)

A delighted Smith turns away after scoring Dundee's second. Ugolini wonders what all the fuss is about.

THE GOAL that beats Celtic—and it's the result of a Dundee "double act." Centre Alan Cousin (not in picture) sends over a perfect cross; inside left Alan Gilzean gets his head to it. The ball flies between Parkhead centre half John McNamee and goalkeeper Frank Haffey. On right: Dundee's Hugh Robertson and Celtic's Pat Crerand.

THE goal that started the rout of Rangers. GILZEAN beats DAVIS in the jump to head into the net, well clear of the desperately-lunging RITCHIE.

Above: The first of Gilzean's four goals against Rangers at Ibrox (61-62). Below: "It's easy for the league leaders!" Dad's shout when Gillie put us in front against Hibs (61-62)

The goal that turned the tide at Easter Road. A spreadeagled RONNIE SIMPSON is unable to reach the Gilzean head that put Dundee in front just before the interval.

MOMENT of rescue for Dundee in 88 minutes at Rugby Park. Kilmarnock keeper Sandy McLaughlan lies on the ground with the ball in his arms after his controversial "save" from an Alan Cousin lob. Dundee's Alan Gilzean and Andy Penman raise their hands to claim a goal. Gordon Smith is in the goal area, Killie's Matt Watson on left. The referee awards a goal—and the league leaders save that precious point.

Phew! That was a close one! Cousin's disputed last minute equaliser against Killie (Feb 62)

Wild celebrations follow Gilzean's winner against United!

ABERDEEN 1 RANGERS 0 | DUNDEE 2 ST. MIRREN 0

● "It's mine," shouts Saints 'keeper Bobby Williamson as he drops to the ground to snatch the ball from Dundee's inrushing Andy Penman. Standing in for Williamson is right-half Rab Stewart.

Left: Tension at Dens as Penman threatens Saint's goal.

Right: Dundee up - Rangers down! Celebrating Dens fans invade the pitch - and prepare for Perth!

DUNDEE UP! RANGERS DOWN!! And joyous Dens Park fans invade the pitch, with high hopes of their first-ever League championship.

TOPPERS!

No slips this time as the Dens Parkers win their first Flag

DUNDEE'S GOLDEN DAY

"We are the champs!" Captain Bobby Cox is hailed by the fans.
Dad and I are there - somewhere!

I've done it again, shouts Alan Gilzean as he beats Muirton 'keeper Bill Taylor and centre-half Ferguson for his second goal to make sure of the Flag and a place in the money making European Cup tourney.

"Take that!" Gillie's goals against the Saints.

No wonder Alan Gilzean is leaping high. He's just put Dundee ahead with the first of their three goals. St. Johnstone's Jim Ferguson can only stand and watch but Andy Penman is ready to rush in and congratulate his team-mate.

Pat Liney was a reliable goalkeeper who was on occasion, outstanding. The fullbacks, Hamilton and Cox, were in my opinion the best in Scotland. "Hammy" was probably the first of his time to be known as an attacking overlapping back and Cox was a great captain, famed for his sliding tackles. Ure was a colossus at centre half and Seith and Wishart provided class in midfield. The forwards were a handful for any team. On the right was Smith, who's guile and crosses for Gilzean were a feature of Dundee's play and on the left, in contrast, Robertson jinked and turned full backs inside out. Penman (who notched 17 goals that season), at only 19, a mixture of pace and power, who along with the magnificent and surely under-rated Alan Cousin (scorer of 15 goals) and of course the deadly Alan Gilzean (who finished top scorer with 24), made a wonderful combination of ariel power and deadly finishing. Brown, McGeachie, Waddell and Stuart were the players who were used on occasion and these guys could have comfortably been first team regulars at most clubs.

Bob Shankly had been an inspirational manager and we shouldn't forget the contribution that coach Sammy Kean and Physiotherapist Lawrie Smith made to the ultimate success of what was a wonderful footballing side. A great team on and off the park.

That was the team that was!!!!!!

Chapter 10

A European Adventure

During the close season Dundee took part in what was at the time a really prestigious tournament in New York called the New York Tourney, competing with teams from Brazil, Italy and Germany. Normally, the invitation to take part was given to the teams who were runners up in their respective leagues and so the SFA, when it seemed likely Dundee were going to finish in the runners up spot, nominated the Dark Blues for a place. The results were not particularly great however; winning one, drawing two, and losing two out of the five games played. However, it gave the team some valuable experience against foreign opposition, which would stand them in good stead in the months to come.

August 11th 1962, Tannadice Park

Dundee United 3 - 2 Dundee

At home, the Clackmannanshire Branch of the Dundee Supporters Club stood at Alloa train station on the first Saturday of the season, waiting to embark on yet another journey to see the Dark Blues.

The Champion's first game was in the League Cup against United, away.

Over 25,000 fans squeezed in to a new look Tannadice, which was now sporting a new L shaped stand. We took our place behind the goal at the shed end. In these days, the teams came out separately and United took to the field first. When Dundee appeared, it seemed as if the whole stadium shook with applause. The crowd at that time must have been at least two-thirds Dundee supporters! The Dundee fans ratio to United became really apparent when "Gillie" rocketed us ahead and the packed crowd behind the goal surged forward in delight. But, typically, United got stuck in and knocked us out of our stride. In an untidy sort of a game, with the match balanced at 2-2 with minutes to go, they notched a late winner, sending us home disappointed (big understatement!). It had been a really poor opening display by the champions. Dundee would have to get used to teams of lesser ability trying to stop them playing the football for which they had become famous.

Oh Bhoy!

All was forgiven though on the following Wednesday however, when Celtic came to town. In front of a 20,000 crowd, the Bhoys were sent packing pointless as a Gordon Smith goal sealed the points for Dundee!

Two defeats in a row to Hearts followed, one of which was the opening League game in defence of the League Crown. The results against Hearts were disappointing and, although we seemed to be playing well enough, the opposition in each game seemed to see Dundee as a scalp to be won and, as a result, appeared to try that bit harder. It was something that Dundee were going to have to get used to. Next was the visit of United in the return League Cup fixture at Dens.

August 25th 1962, Dens Park, League Cup

Dundee 2 - 1 Dundee United

As usual, against Dundee, United worked their socks off but, this time, class told in the end. The Champions turned on the style and, in front of almost 20,000, two goals from 38 year old Gordon Smith gave Dundee a deserved victory. Smith's first goal was as fine a goal as he ever scored in his long illustrious career. It started with a fine pass from Cousin. Smith then took the ball inside, and with everyone expecting a pass he suddenly wheeled and drove a tremendous left footer into the net from twenty-five yards!

In the second half, United, with a strong wind behind them, equalised in forty-nine minutes and for a period were on top. The Champions were struggling to play their passing game in the blustery conditions but their persistence paid off though when, in seventy-eight minutes, young Kenny Cameron crossed from the right and the veteran Smith got to the ball before United's keeper, Donald McKay, to head the ball into the net for the winner!

All Ears!

I was fifteen now and playing regularly at Junior level against guys sometimes more than twice my age!! Getting to see the Dark Blues was very difficult and almost impossible in midweek fixtures as they conflicted with my footballing schedule, so I had to be content listening in for the Dundee result after my games were finished. In the dressing room, I was sometimes too scared to ask the score. "How did Dundee do today?" I would ask nonchalantly, as if I wasn't too bothered, when all the time my stomach was churning!

The next result that I was listening out for was particularly nerve wracking……and surprising to say the least!

September 5th 1962, Dens Park

European Cup, 1st Round

Dundee 8 - 1 Cologne

Two defeats from Celtic and Hearts was not exactly the ideal build up to arguably the biggest game in Dundee's history; the first round of the European Cup!

The national newspapers were hardly giving Dundee much of a chance, stating that, "It would be experience for a provincial club." The West German Champions had been installed as one of the favourites to win the competition and, with Dundee's form of late hardly inspirational, few gave the Dark Blues a chance.

The game kicked off with Kenneth Wolstenholme - the famous BBC commentator - at the mic and 25,000 Dundee fans singing what Wolstenholme described as, "The Dundee song." "Hail, Hail the 'Dee are here!" reverberated around the ground. Then, less than ten minutes after all the singing had commenced, Cologne conceded an own goal! The fans were rapturous. Then, Dens Park went truly wild when Wishart and Robertson added two more! Dundee were rampant and Gilzean and Smith made it 5-0 before half time! The Germans didn't know what had hit them! Their goalkeeper didn't reappear for the second half, blaming a clash with Dundee's Alan Cousin early in the first half as the reason - yeah right.

But there was more misery for the Germans - there was just no stopping the Dens maestros. Penman and another two from Gilzean made it 8-0!! *Eight!!* The Germans had some consolation however, an o.g from Hamilton made it 8-1.

Dad and I, with no knowledge of the score beforehand, watched anxiously, the highlights on *BBC Sportsview*. Dundee 8, Cologne 1!!!!!!!!!!!!! We couldn't believe it! 8-1!!

Cologne publicly had written Dundee off before the match, which made this all the sweeter, and they went on to blame the loss of their keeper for the debacle. What sore losers! In reality, Dundee had blown their opponents away. "Bring on round two!" we thought.

Sandwiched between the return leg in Germany, in front of 18,000, Dundee scraped a draw with Aberdeen at Dens. Bizarre when you think of the hammering they gave Cologne!! A last minute goal from Alan Gilzean gave them a share of the points. And in a visit to Tannadice for the first League derby of the season, a wonderful Alan Cousin goal claimed a point for the champions. United had gone ahead in the eleventh minute but, four minutes later, Dundee equalised. Cousin himself started the move with a pass to Penman, who rolled the ball back to the centre forward, who then thundered a rocket of a shot into the net from twenty yards. According to the *Scotsport* report, it sent a spray of rain over the fans ducking behind the goal!

This had been a battle of the elegant versus the energetic. League Champions Dundee putting on the style, United putting on their dungarees. This fetish that Dundee had for silk hat and tails soccer sometimes riled even their own supporters however. Dundee weren't up for the lofty clearance up field when under pressure. No, the Champions attempted to short pass their way out of even the tightest spot and, although at times the team moved as smoothly as if on roller skates, they always gave the impression that they could overdo it and lose the daftest of goals needlessly. But that was Dundee - soccer subtlety at its best and a delicacy on the eye when in outfield but on occasion, suicidal in and around their own goal. At Dens the following Saturday, Clyde were beaten 2-0. The Dundee players, according to reports, looked to have one eye on the return European Cup match in Cologne the following Wednesday.

September 26th 1962

Mungersdorfer Stadium

Cologne 4 - 0 Dundee

Again, highlights of the match were on *BBC Sportsview* and the living room at 60 Ochil St, Tillicoultry, exuded an extremely tense atmosphere. We still hadn't had an inkling of the final score as we watched.

Cologne were all over us and scoring almost at will. In what seemed to be no time at all, Cologne were 2-0 ahead. Dundee keeper, Bert Slater (sadly no longer with us and with whom I would work in later years), then was stretchered from the pitch, injured. It was pretty clear that the German press had been hyping up the incident at Dens, when the Cologne goalkeeper had been "injured" and so it was no surprise that Bert Slater had come in for such rough treatment. Andy Penman swapped places with Slater and went in goal, with Slater limping on the right wing. But with the score climbing to 3-0 to the Germans and the game looking like sliding away from the Dark Blues, Slater, with head heavily bandaged, dramatically went back between the sticks. The Germans, who had scored earlier from a penalty, were then awarded a second penalty but, thankfully, the ball crashed against the cross bar and back into play. Phew!

A dazed looking Bert Slater provided some heroic and essential saves but was clearly fouled (again) when he conceded Cologne's fourth goal. The minutes ticked by oh so slowly but eventually the final whistle blew. Dundee had won 8-5 on aggregate!

The Caproni living room had been full of anxiety, pressure and suspense and so, finally, my Dad and I could breathe a huge sigh of relief after what seemed to be an eternity of a football match.

However, further drama was to ensue as the Dundee *players* were attacked by hundreds of German *"fans"*. Fortunately though, British Army soldiers, stationed in the Rhine, stepped in to rescue what was developing into an unprecedented and horrific situation.

Manager Bob Shankly refused to the let the team attend the after dinner reception as he felt that his players had been intimated and physically assaulted for most of the game.

September 29th 1962, Ibrox Stadium

Rangers 1 - 1 Dundee

Only three days later, Dundee visited Ibrox. Amazingly, there appeared to be no sign of tiredness from the silky and almost machine like Dark Blues, who were now unbeaten in the last four league visits to Ibrox.

Rangers went ahead, putting one past the reliable Pat Liney, back in goal for the injured Bert Slater. However, much to the delight of a large Dundee following, Robertson capitalised on a mistake by Ranger's full back Shearer to equalise, giving them a share of the points. A fine second half display by the Dark Blues could have seen them leave with a victory though. Once again Rangers had been outplayed by a drawing board Dundee side that seemed to reserve their best performances for the big occasions.

Shaping Up Nicely

Dundee were starting to find a bit of domestic form now, and by the time they travelled to Portugal to play Sporting Club of Lisbon on European Cup duty they were tucked in nicely, only four points behind league leaders Hearts. But strangely, nobody seemed to care. The European Cup was what it was all about.

October 23rd 1962, Estadio Jose Alvalade (1956)

European Cup, 2nd Round, First Leg,

Sporting Club of Lisbon 1 - 0 Dundee

On Wednesday October 23rd, the Dark Blues ran out in Lisbon to take on Sporting Club of Lisbon in round two of football's most prestigious competition. At 60 Ochil St., we once again waited for the result to come through. We had lost 1-0. However, our initial sense of disappointment was tempered with a feeling that we could overturn the deficit at Dens Park in the return leg. Dundee had only lost to a last minute goal which was not a bad result considering that Sporting were a highly rated side. In front of a crowd of 48,000, Dundee had defended for much of the match and although the goal they lost was a bit unfortunate, being so near the end, there was no doubt that the Portuguese Champions had deserved to win and at times had showed real class. However, we felt that we if we could repeat the form we showed against Cologne in the previous round, we could progress to the next stage of the competition.

October 27th 1962, East End Park

Dunfermline Athletic 2 - 0 Dundee

On the following Saturday, a tired looking Dundee lost 2-0 to Dunfermline at East End Park. I had no game that day and travelled

Dad and me leaving to see Dundee - note my Dundee tie!

SAUCHIE STAR TURNS DOWN SENIOR BIDS

By TOMMY WORKMAN

PETER CAPRONI, the 16-year-old right winger of East of Scotland champions Sauchie, has turned down a chance to go to Dunfermline and Dundee.

He has been asked to sign by both clubs, but as he has had only five games with Sachrie he wants to stay put meantime.

Actually, if Sauchie hadn't been hit by injuries, Caproni, good prospect as he is, wouldn't have played even five games.

Team boss Jimmy Millar tells me that he had planned to leave the boy with his juvenile side this season and bring him along gradually.

So I turned down the 'Dee - I think not!! That's me second on the right, front row, for Alloa Athletic (72-73).

Dundee 'keeper Bert Slater brings off a great save from Anderlecht inside-left Van Himst as the Dens men marched to glory last night.

European Cup against Anderlecht at Dens. Dad and I were up a tree behind the terracing when watching the game!

through with Dad to watch the game. Although it was a disappointing result, somehow I didn't really bother too much. Dundee looked a bit disinterested to be honest and, in the wet and rather windy conditions, the "Pars" seemed more up for the match than we were. To be honest, when they took the lead there looked like there was only going to be one winner - and it certainly wasn't us! My mind though, like the team's I think, was fixed on the following Wednesday, when Sporting would visit Dens in the Second Leg of the European Cup.

October 31st 1962, Dens Park

European Cup, 2nd Round, 2nd leg

Dundee 4 - 1 Sporting Club of Lisbon

Dundee fans loved the European nights and over 32,000 roared Dundee on in what was a magnificent game. The skill and prowess from the Dark Blues was overwhelming. This was football at its very best.

Dundee went ahead within fifteen minutes. Gordon Smith popped up in the inside left position and fed the ball through to Gilzean who then cracked the ball into the net from around fifteen yards. Then, just on half time, after a short corner on the right, Gordon Smith crossed and Alan Cousin got to it first to head against the underside of the crossbar and into the net. We were ahead on aggregate.

In the second half, in the fifty-fourth minute, Gilzean scored a third and only six minutes later the big striker completed his hat-trick with another equally brilliant goal, flicking home a Penman pass! (Gilzean's hat-trick made him one of the most feared strikers in Europe!)

They had turned it around! The men from Dens had done what they needed to do! The club even appeared to have new found nationwide respect. Later in the competition when Dundee played and won in Belgium against Anderlecht, Wolstenholme was heard to exclaim, "I've never seen a British team play football like this before!" Praise indeed!

Getting Closer

I couldn't believe that we were in the Quarter Finals of the European Cup! The final that year was to be at Wembley and Dad and I had already sussed out arrangements to travel to London should we get to the final. The final of the European Cup!!?? Were these words really coming out of my mouth??? Could this be real???!!

The European nights, however, had a down side as the team's domestic form suffered somewhat. Although Airdrie were beaten 2-1 with goals from Gilzean and Houston (I managed to go and see that game) and a 0-0 draw was gained at Celtic Park, there were defeats; Partick Thistle and Third Lanark being the culprits. So by the time Queen of the South visited Dens Park on the 1st December, Dundee were well off the pace in the race for the Championship......or so it seemed.

December 1st 1962, Dens Park

Dundee 10 - 2 Queen of the South

Queen of the South were always a "stuffy" side, difficult to beat. But on this occasion, Dundee raised their game to European standard and ran out winners by **10**-2! Alan Gilzean netted *seven* times that day and by all accounts could have had more. Goals from Penman, Houston and a rare counter from George Ryden sealed the "Doonhamer's" fate. Dundee, incredibly, were 7-2 up at half-time and although George Farm in Queens goal was injured trying to save Dundee's second goal, in truth, no 'keeper could have stopped Dundee that day. The Dark Blues were rampant and it was a warning to all that an on form Dundee team was just about unstoppable.

I was playing for my local junior team, Sauchie, that day (I was trying to develop a career in the beautiful game and one national paper quoted that I had turned down the opportunity of signing for Dundee - as if!! No idea where that came from!!) and I can remember being told the score as I left the dressing room after the game. I couldn't wait to get home to try and catch *Sports Report* on the radio!

However, our inconsistent form on the domestic front continued. St. Mirren and Raith Rovers were beaten 3-0 and 4-2 respectively but then came a draw against Motherwell, a 1-0 New Year's Day defeat to Aberdeen, and a 3-2 home defeat at the hands of Clyde. Our title challenge had effectively, ended.

The Scottish Cup

Following Dundee makes you wary of any sort of prediction. The papers had installed Dundee as second favourites to win the trophy but when the draw was announced that we had Inverness Caley, then of the Highland League, I almost broke out in a sweat! Thoughts of Fraserburgh and Berwick Rangers immediately came rushing back. Surely not again, I thought!

I needn't have worried though. On Jan 12th 1963 at a snow bound Inverness, Dundee, in all white, gave a masters performance to outclass their Highland League opponents to win 5-1.

The weather had been horrendous with heavy snow causing havoc with fixtures all over Britain - and there was no letting up in the conditions. It got even worse over the next few weeks and there was no further football played until February 5th, when it was time for the Scottish Cup tie against Montrose, who had a young Gordon Wallace in their line up. However, the dens men were rampant and crushed the "Gable Endies" in an 8-0 win.

The terrible snowy and wintry conditions continued though, and so by the time Dundee were due to play the first leg of the Quarter Final of The European Cup against Anderlecht in Belgium on March 6th, the Dark Blues had not played a competitive fixture since Feb 5th.

March 6th 1963
European Cup Quarter Final
60 Ochil Street, Tillicoultry & Heysel Stadium, Belgium
Anderlecht 1 - 4 Dundee

The Belgian side had put out Real Madrid in the previous round and the 'Dee were given little chance by many of the so-called "experts" of the time. But Dundee finished up giving one of the best displays in their history.

The game was only sixty seconds old when Gilzean finished a wonderful passing movement with a magnificent right foot shot into the Anderlecht net. Dundee were off to a dream start. Dundee's man-to-man passing was a joy to watch and this was aptly demonstrated in the build up to their second goal. Cousin,

Robertson and Gilzean all exchanged passes before Gilzean struck a twenty yard shot passed a well-beaten Belgian ‘keeper. 2-0.

The Belgian Champions soon put Dundee under tremendous pressure however when they pulled one back from the penalty spot. In the second half though, Alan Cousin eased their duress with a third goal and then Smith, using all of his experience, netted a fourth!

A 60,000 crowd, despite the disappointment that most had of their team being well beaten, sportingly gave the Dundee team a standing ovation after the game. Anderlecht, it must be remembered, were no fools. As mentioned before, they had knocked out Real Madrid in the previous round and Real had won the tournament no fewer than five times! This performance had the National Press predicting that perhaps Dundee could actually win the tournament!! Changed days indeed!

But what goes up must come down. Nothing was truer than that saying for a Dundee fan at that time. I was on a high from that game but was soon brought back down to earth with an almighty bump when coming out of the dressing room at Sauchie the following Saturday, I learned that we had lost 1-0……at Airdrie! How does that even compute?!

March 13th 1963, Dens Park

European Cup Quarter Final, 2nd leg

Dundee 2 - 1 Anderlecht

It was my Dad's birthday, so he was hoping for a present from Dundee. We still hadn't a car so we booked seats on a bus that the local Alloa Y.M.C.A. were organising to go to the match (I used to play for the Y.M. and Alan Cousin used to coach the team on a Thursday evening). Although Dad and I were the only true Dundee fans on that bus, there was no lack of support for the Dark Blues from the people with whom we were travelling.

It was, however, becoming pretty clear that we would be struggling to get to Dens by kick off time. The traffic from Perth to Dundee had been heavy and very slow, and the bus sometimes even stopped for what seemed like an age. Arriving behind schedule and queuing outside Dens at the T.C Key end, we frustratingly had to listen to the roars of the crowd as the teams emerged on to the pitch. I had looked forward to the match all week and now I feared that I might not even get into the stadium!

It was an all ticket match, and although the official attendance was 40,000 it seemed that many more had managed to somehow gain access. When we eventually got through the turnstile at the TC Key end, we were met by hundreds of fans, saying that they couldn't get on to the terracing behind the goal. It could have been a recipe for disaster from a safety aspect, and certainly from a personal point a view, a disaster in that we might not see the match at all! However, Dad wasn't to be denied.

We managed, just, to squeeze into the body of the crowd - but were unable to see any of the pitch! Then came Dad's masterstroke. He spied a tree behind the terracing and, as quick as a flash, we were both climbing up it. Minutes later, we had a bird's eye view of Dens Park!! As we clung on, Dad's words could never have sounded more apt., "We must be daft!" More supporters followed our genius and clambered up the tree too, some even higher than us!

Let The Game Begin!

The Belgian side looked in control and went ahead in the first half after twenty-nine minutes. At this stage, we thought that if Anderlecht scored again then we would have our hands full to hold out and our dream could be over. However, as half time approached it was evident that Dundee were getting to grips with the game and they were denied what looked like a stone wall penalty claim when Robertson was blatantly pushed by Plaskaie in the penalty box. Then, just on half time, 'keeper Trappenier could only touch a Cousin shot onto the bar and Gilzean only just failed to get his head to the rebound.

In the second half, Dundee upped the tempo and put the Belgian side under considerable pressure. Right away Gordon Smith came close to scoring on two occasions - this made the tree sway! Then, Alex Hamilton hit a glorious twenty yarder only to see the Belgian 'keeper pull off an incredible save. In fifty-nine minutes, the 'keeper dived to save from Penman and a free kick from the same player was deflected inches wide. Dundee were on the rampage! Then, with only ten minutes left, Alan Cousin equalised! A Gordon Smith cross was headed out and the big centre forward steadied and took a touch before shooting home from the edge of the box! The tree was only just surviving - and its roots were given the ultimate test just only minutes later.

With only six minutes remaining, Robertson made a run up the left and crossed low to Gordon Smith, who seemed to lose his chance as he dragged the ball into the defence. But then he quickly switched the ball to his left foot and shot for goal, resulting in the ball cannoning in off the far post for a glorious winner! It was pandemonium all around us! The tree shook violently as the rambunctious fans celebrated! Dad and I did well to hang on! Some weren't so lucky though and came tumbling down past us - but they didn't seem to mind; the joy replaced the pain!! The roars from the ground that day were apparently heard as far away as the harbour - two miles away!

Afterwards, Eugene Steppe, boss of Anderlecht commented, **"Dundee are a better side than Real Madrid."** Joseph Jurion, capped forty times for Belgium said, **"Dundee are the best club side that I have ever seen - I can't see anyone stopping Dundee winning the Cup - not even Benfica."** (How I wish people were saying that in the year 2009)

Dundee were through to the Semi Final of The European Cup!

Back To Auld Claes And Porridge

Three days later it was back to the bread and butter of the League. Partick Thistle visited Dens Park and a young Kenny Cameron scored the winner to give Dundee the points. It maybe wasn't as exciting as the previous match but we were on a roll!

March 18th 1963, Dens Park, Scottish Cup, 3rd Round

Dundee 1 - 0 Hibs

I was playing somewhere near Edinburgh and near to the end of my match I was desperate to find out what the score was at Dens. It was about a couple of minutes to go and I was about to take a corner kick. As I was placing the ball, I quickly asked a fan if he knew the score with Hibs. "Heard it was 1-0," he replied. I then quickly had to return my attention to my own match but shouted out of the side of my mouth, "1-0 - who for?" (It was a good job I scored three goals that day otherwise I might have been given a little bit of "stick" from my manager!) I took the corner and the final whistle blew. The crowd then started to dissipate and I was trying to grab the attention of the guy who had been standing at the corner flag. But he never heard my shout. This was agony now. But I needn't have worried. Dad, who had been standing at the other side of the pitch, had walked round to the entrance to the dressing rooms. "Gilzean, 1-0," was all he said! Dundee were through to the Quarter Finals of the Scottish Cup!

Dundee could realistically win the European and Scottish Cups……someone pinch me!

Chapter 11

The End Of The Adventure

With Dundee now in the Semi Final of the European Cup and the Quarter Final of the Scottish Cup, I was getting used to seeing my favourites occupy prime editing space in the National Press. However, the Dark Blues appeared to be reserving their best performances for what was considered "big cup" competitions and their league form was less than inspiring.

After knocking Hibs out of the Cup, a 4-1 defeat at Celtic Park was hardly the confidence booster for their forthcoming Quarter Final tie with Rangers at Dens Park.

March 30th 1963, Dens Park
Scottish Cup Quarter Final
Dundee 1 - 1 Rangers

'Almost 37,000 see the "big two" serve up an, "uninspiring match",' one national newspaper commented. I think that with so much at stake, and the fact that both teams had such huge respect for each other, the normal attacking flair from both teams was contained a little. Both goals had come from penalties; Dundee's scorer being Andy Penman, who slotted home his spot kick in his usual efficient manner.

April 3rd 1963, Ibrox Stadium, Scottish Cup Replay

Rangers 3 - 2 Dundee

In the replay at Ibrox, I listened in to the radio. With playing regularly myself, and Dad following me around the country, getting to see my team in the flesh was still proving difficult but it certainly didn't make me any less fervent in my support for Dundee FC. In fact, on the contrary. I savoured every single snippet of information that I could read about my team and listened in every week for the result as if my life depended on the outcome.

The replay was a game that saw Dundee lead 2-1 with only fifteen minutes left, only to get sloppy, however, and lose two late goals. Rangers had initially led thanks to an own goal from Hamilton but Gilzean scored twice to put Dundee on top before Rangers equalised with a disputed penalty. Then, the Ibrox men got the winner late in the game and there was just no way back for Dundee. The crowd had been an incredible 82,000 and it was a game in which Dundee was the better side and should have won. But we didn't - and we were out. The dream of the double was no more. I was, as the saying goes, as sick as a parrot!!

More Misfortune

The build up to the Semi Final of the European Cup could not have been less inspiring. The Dark Blues recorded only one win out of five and, despite hitting five against St. Mirren, they still very annoyingly lost to United at Dens, 2-1.

April 24th 1963, San Siro Stadium

European Cup Semi Final, 1st leg

AC Milan 5 - 1 Dundee

Viewed From: 60 Ochil Street, Tillicoultry

With the exception of perhaps Cup Finals or Internationals, it was unusual for any other game to be televised live in these times so it was a surprise when we learned that the second half of the match in Milan was going to be televised live on *BBC Sportsview*!

The match was all that I could think about that day and we were delighted when the programme - *at last* - commenced and even more so when we learned that it was 1-1. Alan Cousin, mid way through the first half, equalised the loss of an early Milan goal, making him the first Scottish player ever to score at the San Siro. The commentator was singing the praises of Dundee's first half performance and so we had high hopes of coming away still in the competition!

In the second half though, Milan opened strongly and went 3-1 ahead but both goals, in my opinion, should have been disallowed. When the second Milan goal went in, the ball appeared to be over the bye line by some margin before the cross came in and the third goal was clearly offside; a Milan forward appeared to be standing on the Dundee goal line as the ball went in the net! The referee initially seemed to be disallowing the goal but then changed his mind after consulting the linesman who had actually run onto the pitch to make his point. Before the two Milan counters, ironically, Dundee could have and probably should have gone ahead when Doug Houston found himself with only the goalkeeper to beat but missed the target. Then, further disaster struck. Bert Slater in the Dundee goal had been surrounded with Italian photographers standing behind his goal and their constant flashing of flash bulbs made it even more difficult for the Dundee 'keeper to command his area and so in the last quarter we lost a further two goals.

The Dundee defence, normally so strong, and so cool under pressure, seemed to be unsettled by the Italians and it ended 5-1. The referee, however, came in for some severe criticism. Later it was recorded that he had received expensive jewellery from Milan before the match and whether there was any truth in the rumour I have no idea but he was later, as I understand, banned by the governing authorities of the day for other bribery charges. There was no doubt that Dundee had been harshly treated by the officials. It looked, and felt like, that it was all over.

May 1st 1963, Dens Park

2nd leg, European Cup Semi Final

Dundee 1 - 0 AC Milan

Dad and I got tickets for the match and travelled to Dens in a friend's car. The atmosphere was electric as 38,000 fans roared on the Dark Blues who were in their change strip of all white. At that time, both Dundee's home and change strip looked sheer class. The Dark Blue shirt with the big white D.F.C. badge was quality, and when the team wore their change strip of all white they just exuded class.

It was all Dundee but the Italians were masters at defending and they slowed down the game at every opportunity. With only minutes to go to half time though, the dead lock was broken as Gilzean majestically headed home a cross from Gordon Smith to make it 1-0!

After the interval, the Italians tried every dirty trick in the book and the game was starting to get a bit "untidy" to say the least. However, soon after the second half started, the crowd erupted when Penman netted! The goal however, was disallowed for offside against Gilzean, which I still hotly dispute to this day. I was in the stand enclosure, directly in line with Gilzean, and I honestly saw nothing to convince me that the goal should not have stood. But yes, then again, I could be accused of being a little biased!

Then, Dundee should have been awarded a penalty when Smith was nothing less than assaulted in the box. The game just kept getting more temperamental and eventually boiled over in the latter stages when Gilzean was ordered off for retaliation. Though I could never condone a player for lashing out, I have to say that I had great sympathy for "Gillie" as the tackle on him was quite disgraceful and could have crippled him, had he not managed to avoid it. It was quite ironic that it was a Dundee player that was sent off as Gilzean, and perhaps even more so, Gordon Smith, who actually at one stage was punched in the face, had been the subject of brutal treatment at the hands of the Italian side all evening.

And so it was all over. The final whistle blew and Dundee were out. The Wembley final was tailor made for Dundee as well and I would have backed my team against anyone in Europe if we had made it through. But it was not to be.

Back To Basics

May 18th 1963, Brockville Park

Falkirk 0 - 2 Dundee

With the season effectively over, we travelled to Falkirk for the second last game. In the five games up to this one, we won twice, lost once and drew once. But really, it was anti-climax stuff now.

We watched as Gilzean and Smith scored to win the points in front of only 2,000 at Brockville. Dundee coasted through the game and looked, to be honest, as if they were in "third gear" for much of it, raising their game only when necessary.

In the final game at Dens before 17,000, the Champions played the new Champions, Rangers, drawing 0-0.

But what a journey we had been on. It was a season never to be forgotten and full of wonderful memories. Dundee had shaken European football to its very core and the name of Dundee F.C. was now known well outside the boundaries of the team's Scottish heritage.

Ominously though, for the first time in their history, Dundee United finished higher up the league than their more esteemed neighbours from Dens Park. However, I didn't think too much about that at the time as I felt that Dundee's league form had had the distraction of the European Cup and the league table was a bit false. Hmm, I was getting good at consoling myself! However, in the next two seasons we would again finish above United in the league. But it was getting more difficult.

Chapter 12

And What About The Fans?

When writing this book, I pondered about just how important football really is? Is it really as important as life itself? Or, as famously put by Bill Shankly, "*More* important"?

Of course it isn't. There is, however, no doubt that it plays an integral part in the everyday lives of ordinary football fans everywhere. When Sunderland last won the FA Cup, apparently productivity went up in the area by around 20%. And there is no doubt that when Dundee wins, I am a completely different person to that than when they lose - and my wife is testimony to that!

In the season 07-08, when we hung on to Hamilton's coattails for so long but finished up being runners up, I remember travelling back from the game at Hamilton with my friend Bruce Porter (I got friendly with Bruce, whilst sitting next to him in the South Enclosure every second week and we decided to share a car to away trips). We discussed the game from start to finish, resulting in me feeling pretty depressed as we had lost 2-0, so that Saturday evening I was never going to be great company. However, my wife had arranged for our good friends, Bruce and Diane Peggie, to come over for dinner and later that night, during the meal, I suddenly felt this kick under the table. It was then that I realised that I had disassociated myself from the general conversation and was away in a world of my own, thinking about the game. My wife indicated later that I actually at one point "tutted" and shook my head in disgust!! So, sorry to our friends!

To demonstrate my point further, my mind rolls back to a game between Hearts and Dundee on a Wednesday night: March 12th, 1969. Both clubs were sitting in mid table, and to everybody else outside those with Hearts and Dundee persuasions it was really a meaningless fixture. The game actually should have been played in January but in fact wasn't because the clubs were involved in a Scottish Cup match against each other, which we lost 2-1.

Dad and I had - against our better judgement - decided to travel through to the match at Tynecastle. I say against our better judgement simply because the weather was quite abysmal. In fact, the prediction was heavy snow, and as soon as we left our house at Tillicoultry the snow was already threatening.

When we arrived at Tynecastle the weather had worsened quite considerably and the snow was substantial but as yet not lying on the wet roads. We quickly made our way into the stadium and into the covered terracing that used to be on the popular side at Tynecastle, where now stands an impressive 6,000 seater stand. Tynecastle was a different place in these days. No all seated accommodation then and, of course, no segregation either.

The snow was now even heavier and, as the teams ran out, we suddenly realised that we were surrounded by Hearts fans. It seemed as if we were the only Dundee supporters there! My Dad, I felt, was indeed justified when he came out with his now special cliché of, "We must be daft." It was unbelievably cold and it didn't help when Hearts soon scored and then added another just before half time. Even the half time Bovril, normally so welcome, didn't do much to make us feel any better.

We walked along the enclosure near to the end where Dundee would be attacking in the second half, away from the Hearts fans - away from everybody if the truth be told. It was turning out to be a dire game. My attention drifted to the snow that was swirling in the sky, in big flakes, somehow never seeming to land. We were literally freezing and the wind was bitter. But then, something happened which changed everything - we scored! Jocky Scott was the scorer, making it 2-1.

Jocky Scott - the present manager of our team (2009) - was some player. The site of Jocky, head down, holding on to his sleeve cuffs and running at defenders, was a joy to behold. Without doubt, Jocky, along with Cannigia and Alan Cousin, is the best runner with the ball I have ever seen in a Dark Blue shirt. Jocky used to run *at* opponents with the ball. He was a hugely exciting player.

To be honest, I can't remember too much about how Jocky's goal went in but it sure changed the whole pattern of the match. It was still raw but we didn't feel it. Dundee actually looked like they might just equalise. "C'mon the 'Dee!" we shouted.

Then, in the last minute, Alex Kinninmonth squeezed the ball in at the back post for an equaliser! Dad and I were ecstatic! It finished 2-2 but if felt like a victory. We stayed to cheer the team from the pitch and one or two of the players even gave us a wave!

On the way back, Dad and I talked about the game as if we had just won the cup! It sure is a funny old game. On waking the next morning the first thing that came into my mind was Dundee's equalising goal and I smiled. That goal made me so happy that my good spirits continued into the following day!

Why The 'Dee?

Yep, the beautiful game plays a bigger part in football fan's lives than perhaps we realise but what really makes someone follow Dundee FC? At the moment (2009) with the side in Scotland's second tier, being a Dundee fan is a bit of a penance! So there must be a deep fondness and attachment involved to continue to follow Dundee - or any inconsistent team for that matter; something that most of the players of the clubs don't have, as they come and go in their hordes. I read recently, in Adrian Chiles excellent book, "We Don't Know What We're Doing," about his experiences following West Bromwich Albion, and one of the things he mentions is that it seems to be clear that players don't really love the club as much as the fans.

Having played at professional level, I agree with this. When I played for the Albion or Alloa, I wanted to win as much as anybody but I could never ever say that I really *loved* the club. When I stopped playing, I rejoined the Albion backroom team and then moved onto other clubs, but came back to the Albion again, after my time at Aberdeen, to set up their Youth Policy, and so in total, spent over twenty years at the club. But even though I always had huge affection for them, and their supporters, the only club that I can honestly say that I have ever really *loved*, is Dundee - but that's because I am a supporter. If you have supported the club and then go onto play for them, then that's different of course.

The Glory Hunters

Living in the central belt I can think of many who support the Old Firm, basically because they win trophies on a regular basis, I suppose. Certainly, I could never be accused of being a glory hunter in the choice of club I support! Although, back in the sixties, long before football tops and scarves were on show in the big stores, I remember seeing a Dundee scarf in a shop window in Alloa and even remember seeing the odd scarf being sported by guys that had no connection with Dundee. So I suppose success attracts fans who are maybe a bit lukewarm in their enthusiasm.

When I was at school, most of my mates supported the Old Firm teams. It was a shock if you met a boy in my area similar in age that supported Dundee, and when you lived as far away from Dundee as I did you rarely, if ever, met another Dundee fan. I remember however, when I was about ten, kicking a ball about outside my house when I was suddenly aware of another boy, slightly older than I was, standing watching. I hadn't seen him before and it turned out that he was visiting his Aunt who lived a few doors up. We got chatting and I asked him if he liked football and when he replied that he did I asked him which team he supported. "I support

Dundee," he said. Shocked to the core I ran inside, shouting to my Dad, "Dad, Dad, I've just met another Dundee supporter!"

The Old Firm

Rangers were the team that won most trophies in the mid Fifties and so I suppose Celtic fans of the same age group as me might have been tempted to complain to the "Almighty" as well as they didn't exactly set the heather on fire either, winning only one trophy from 1954 right up until 1965, when they beat Dunfermline to win the Scottish Cup. However, in 1957 they beat Rangers 7-1 at Hampden in the final of the League Cup, which I'm sure was enough to keep any "hoops" fan going! What I would give to see Dundee beat United 7-1 in a cup final!! It would certainly keep *me* going for a long time and I would gladly, at this very moment, take that and twenty barren years to follow!!

But to be a real Dundee fan, you need plenty of resilience and, above all, a sense of humour!

I remember thinking just how unlucky I had been as I started supporting the team in 1954, just after they had, in the previous five years, won the League Cup twice in succession and were runners up in the League and Scottish Cup. I missed seeing the legendary Billy Steel and the famous teams that brought League Cup success.

However, I realise now, when I speak to younger fans, that I have actually been very lucky indeed. I have had the pleasure of seeing Dundee F.C. when they arguably had the best side the club ever had, in seasons 1961-62 and 62-63.

A Deafening Endorsement

Nowadays (2009), I think that we have a pretty noisy away support. It's funny how the away support of any club always seems to be noisier than a home support. Maybe it's got something to do with being outnumbered and therefore looking on yourselves as the underdog. This, I think, is the case now when Dundee meet United. I think our support always seems to outshout United - which wasn't always the case. Just after United gained promotion in 1959-60, when the teams met, even though almost two thirds of the crowd were sporting Dark Blue, the United fans made the most noise and the "Tannadice Howl", as it was named, was something of which they were rightly proud.

In contrast, the Dundee fans of that era, in most derby matches, seemed content to wait until we scored before making any noise. It was and still is about levels of expectation though and that is why sometimes, at home games, the Old Firm suffer from it as well.

There appears to be a lack of atmosphere until we or indeed the opposition, score.

Black Cats And Ladders

Yes, football is a funny old game, especially when it involves superstition. I have three different Dundee scarves. If Dundee won at a certain venue when I've worn a particular scarf, I cannot possibly go to the match wearing anything else but that particular scarf! And it's the same if we lose. I take a mental note about what I was wearing. At away games, if we get a result I even leave home early so that I can park my car in the same parking spot.

At school, when I was really young and just learning the hard way about what supporting Dundee was all about, I used to flick through a book and stop randomly. If Dundee were playing away from home that weekend, if the page stopped at say, page 52, it would mean that they would lose 5-2 but if it stopped at page 25 it would mean that they would win 2-5! Was I paranoid? Hmm, no. A tad OCD? Perhaps. Daft then? Most likely!

Of course it's not just supporters that are superstitious. Former United manager, Alex Smith, is the most superstitious person I have ever met. I worked with Alex for twelve years at Stirling Albion and another couple at Aberdeen when he was in charge of the Dons along with Jocky Scott. One Saturday springs to mind when I was with Stirling Albion and Alex was manager. Stirling Albion were due to travel to play Kilmarnock in a First Division fixture and the First Division that season had teams like Motherwell, Falkirk, Dunfermline and, of course, Kilmarnock in it and, just as it is today, it was a very competitive League.

The Albion had a really decent side and we had been on a fine run of about five games without defeat and, travelling to the match in the team coach, Alex had made the point to his assistant George Peebles and me that in every game where we had worn white socks, we had never lost. When we arrived at Rugby Park, in passing the home dressing room, Alex noticed that some of the Killie players were ready to go out for a warm up and......horror.....*they* were wearing white socks which would mean that *we* would have to wear our change socks of red. In the away dressing room Alex called me aside and asked me to go along to the Killie dressing room to tell them that we had only white socks with us, so could they change? I did so with some trepidation and I can assure you that the Killie players and staff were far from happy but, under duress, they agreed to change! On my return Alex was estatic, “Yes!” he exclaimed. “Well done wee man, we’ll definitely get a result now!” We got a result alright - just not a very good one - we got stuffed 5-0!

Going back to football supporters I suppose most fans have their little superstitions, they help you just to get by from week to week. But I guess fans of the Old Firm don't really have to have as many little quirks and qualms. Ahh, how nice that would be! But to be really honest, I couldn't be bothered supporting either of the big two. Where would the fun be? Most weeks the Old Firm win anyway. Supporting Dundee is an experience, full of ups and downs. Yes, of course it would be nice to follow a team that won more often than not and so was less likely to break your heart, but it's the unknowing of Dundee's fortunes that keep you on your toes, no matter where they are in the league or what stage the game is at.

When you are winning 1-0 with only five minutes to go, it's a torturous affair. Something deep inside keeps alerting you that something awful is about to happen, and when it does it's just too heartbreaking to put into words. However, and I'm no sadist, but that kind of distress at least makes you feel alive!!

But why does that happen so often? Just when you are in touching distance of victory, the enemy snatches it from within your grasp and devastates you by clinching a last minute/second goal. I am certain that most supporters of provincial clubs will agree with me - particularly when you play either half of the Old Firm - that if you're winning with only minutes to go, your anxiety actually seems to translate onto the players. Just how many times do the really traditionally great sides like Celtic, Rangers and Man. United score a winner or equaliser in the final minutes of a game?

Quite simply I think it is because they believe that they will and supporters like us almost invariably believe that we are going to lose a goal and, hey, what do you know - we do! Their supporters believe that they won't lose either whereas its part of the makeup of a Dundee fan to believe the opposite. Look for the worst and then you will never be disappointed!

I remember playing for the Albion against Rangers at Annfield Park, Stirling Albion's old ground, and we were winning 1-0 with around seven minutes to go, when the ball went out of play. I went to the front of the old stand at Annfield to retrieve it and there was this little lad with a big red and white scarf on, sitting with his Dad. He threw the ball back onto the track but it was the look of fear in his eyes that stayed with me (a look that I now recognise in myself when I watch Dundee!). Even at that young age he probably knew that disaster was about to happen. He was right. We lost 2-1!

Sometimes we turn the world upside down though - and that is when it is all worthwhile! I guess that's my whole point, in that Rangers and Celtic fans experience less turbulence and so therefore, I conclude, it must be so boring being a Rangers or Celtic fan!! We are much more easily pleased too. We are delighted winning two in a row whereas, if you support the Old Firm and if you don't win every week, your world is in crisis.

You Are My Dundee, My Super Dundee!

Following the 'Dee (the club appears to be known as the "Dees" now but in the sixties it was always just the 'Dee) is not something that should be undertaken if you want an easy life! Partick Thistle are labelled by the West of Scotland press as the "great unpredictables" of the Scottish game but, arguably, that mantle lies with us.

But for all that, I wouldn't have it any other way. I mean, what could replace the feeling of going away from home and winning when you are expected to lose? It's great being chuffed to bits, driving home, and looking forward to your Saturday evening meal with a bottle of red wine after that happens. And of course, in defeat, a glass or two of vino helps the "sick as a parrot" feeling turn to one of hope for next week. When you support Dundee, there is always next week!

Chapter 13

Up For The Cup

The 1963-64 season began in fine fashion. In the League Cup campaign, we overcame a tricky opening fixture at Cathkin against Third Lanark, with Cousin and Gilzean netting in a 2-1 win. Next up was Airdrie at Dens and goals from Penman and Houston saw off the Lanarkshire side. With two wins out of two, Dad and I travelled to Dens for the visit of Dunfermline - but this time - in our *own* car! Dad had just bought a split new Morris 1100 for £644....yes, *£644*!

August 17th 1963, Dens Park

Dundee 4 - 1 Dunfermline Athletic

We stood half way up a packed south enclosure and witnessed a vintage Dundee performance in which Andy Penman was outstanding. A Championship winner when he was only 19, he was now maturing into a great, all round player. Before a crowd of 17,000, he scored twice in a 4-1 win. At centre half for Dundee was George Ryden who had replaced the fans favourite Ian Ure, who would shortly be on his way to Arsenal for £62,500. Gilzean and

Robertson completed the scoring in a fine win for a Dundee side that looked eager to add to the glories of the last two seasons. On the form displayed against the Fifers, they looked a side well capable of winning a major honour.

The sun shining, we departed Dens Park in Dad's brand new car, gleaming in the sunlight. On our way back home, we stopped at Auchtermuchty and indulged ourselves with a fish supper. It had been a great day out. A 4-1 victory and now we were tucking into some fish and chips! For what more could we ask?!

August 21st 1963, Dens Park

Dundee 1 - 1 Rangers

The following Wednesday, Rangers were visitors to Dens in the opening fixture of the League Campaign. Another huge crowd of 34,500 turned out and observed a 1-1 draw. A rare goal from Bobby Seith gave Dundee a share of the points, but by all accounts the Dens men should have taken the spoils. Rangers had taken the lead with a first half penalty but Bobby Seith's equaliser was something special. Over twenty- five yards out, the ex-Burnley mid fielder took a touch to control the ball before rifling an unstoppable shot into the Rangers net. Seith was a cultured type of player who always seemed to have time on the ball and, although he wasn't famed for his goal-scoring prowess, the Dundee midfielder became the darling of the Dundee fans that night. It was in fact only Seith's fourth goal since joining the club, the last one being against Dunfermline the previous season, but it had been worth waiting for!

Then, back in the League Cup, in the corresponding home fixture against Third Lanark, in front of almost 15,000, a Gilzean hat-trick saw off the Hi Hi's in a 3-2 Dens win! However, in typical Dundee fashion, an unexpected 4-1 reverse at Airdrie dented our growing confidence. This result meant that we *had* to win at Dunfermline to qualify for the next stage of the competition. Travelling to Dunfermline in the last sectional game was nerve-wracking, knowing that a defeat would see us - despite our fine start - go out of the competition. But we needn't have worried.

August 31st 1963, East End Park, League Cup

Dunfermline Athletic 3 - 4 Dundee

East End Park was always difficult for visiting sides and this game was no different. Dundee, however, were beginning to show a resilience that previous Dundee sides may have lacked. Despite the Fife side pushing them all the way, Dundee showed a lot of battling qualities and this, allied to their classy football, was making the Dens Parkers a very difficult side to play against. Whenever it seemed Dunfermline looked like taking control, Dundee seemed to up the tempo and, in the end, deserved to win a match that had been exciting from start to finish. Gilzean notched twice for the

Dens Parkers and an emerging Kenny Cameron weighed in with a brace as well to seal the Pars' fate.

In the second game of the League Campaign, Dundee travelled to Pittodrie. Aberdeen were a "stuffy" side in these days but no more than that and we hoped that Dundee's class would tell. For once we were right. Aberdeen 2, Dundee 4. Three points from our first two games meant that we were on Rangers' coat tails at the top the league!

September 11th 1963, Dens Park
League Cup Quarter Final, 1st leg
Dundee 3 - 3 Hibs

In the League Cup, Dad and I, and 25,000 others, witnessed a real classic. It really was a super game of football with both teams going all out to attack. However, despite goals from Gilzean, Penman and Waddell, and looking much the better side, in typical Dundee fashion, we still managed to throw the game away. Slack defensive work on several occasions let Hibs back into the game and the Easter Road side took full advantage to equalise. The game should have been dead and buried long before Hib's comeback.

Easter Eggsit

September 18th 1963, Easter Road

League Cup Quarter Final, 2nd leg

Hibs 2 - 0 Dundee

In the second leg at Easter Road, we saw our team lose 2-0 in front of 30,000. It was a tie that we should have won but so typical of Dundee that they didn't. The real Dundee just never turned up that night and it was most frustrating. Hibs, although deserving to win, really had been pretty ordinary. We were more annoyed than disappointed and to this day the thought of that game still brings out feelings of frustration. Again we had been the better side for much of the match but never seemed to get a break in front of goal, and just when it seemed we were in the ascendency we were slack at the back and lost two goals that might have been avoided. On the way back to our car I was really cheesed off to say the least. It wasn't so much that we had lost; it was the fact that we really could have and should have won.

September 14th 1963, Dens Park

Dundee 1 - 1 Dundee United

Sandwiched in between the two Hibs ties was the first derby of the season. It was against United at Dens. Before 22,000, myself included, we drew 1-1, with Gilzean notching his customary goal.

It was a game of contrasting styles; Dundee persevering with their more studied approach whilst United kept up an amazing tempo of pressing the ball to stop their more talented neighbours getting into their stride. On leaving Dens, I was gutted that we didn't win but, in a way, relieved that at least we hadn't lost. Losing to United was and still is the worst feeling in the world for me, and thousands of fellow 'Dees, so sometimes a draw is acceptable. I kept telling myself on the way home that we really should have won though!

In the next three fixtures, Dundee beat Third Lanark, East Stirling and Queen of the South - hammering the latter 5-0 at Palmerston. However, a 3-1 reverse at home to Motherwell saw Dundee suffer their first league defeat of the season.

October 19th 1963, Easter Road

Hibs 0 - 4 Dundee

My game was off due to a waterlogged pitch so Dad and I decided to drive to Easter Road, hoping to see Dundee gain revenge for their League Cup exit at the hands of the "Hibees". The Hibs defeat in the League Cup really rankled and I was desperate to see Dundee put the Edinburgh side to the sword.

The first half ended 0-0 with Dundee the more likely side but their play had lacked a cutting edge - but what a transformation in the second half.

Dundee's first goal came in the fifty-sixth minute when Cousin's headed pass caught the Hib's defence sleeping and "Gillie" hammered the ball home from around eighteen yards. Then, in the sixty-seventh minute, a Waddell cross was nodded back by Robertson and, again, it was Gilzean who was on the spot to crack the ball home.

Just ten minutes later, in the seventy-seventh minute, came Gilzean's hat-trick, and arguably the best of all the goals. Chasing a through ball from Smith, the lanky striker left two defenders in his wake before sending a diagonal overhead shot right into the Hib's net! What an amazing goal! Then, in the last minute, Dundee were awarded a penalty after a Robertson shot was armed away by a Hibs defender. Gilzean's spot-kick was parried by goalkeeper Simpson, but "Gillie" followed up to net his fourth! THAT, I thought, was what should have happened in the League Cup game. I was happy enough to accept it right now though!

Alan Gilzean, Goal Machine!

Alan Gilzean. I first heard that name when Bob Shankly mentioned him when talking to my father, when I was training at Dens as a thirteen year old. The first time I saw "Gillie" in action was at Dens in the season 1959-60 against Stirling Albion, when he scored a hat-trick in a 4-1 win. Over the next four seasons the name "Gilzean" was seldom out of the headlines. He will be remembered for his wonderful performances in the European Cup, but probably most of all for his four goals at Ibrox in the historic 5-1 win in Dundee's championship winning season.

Although he was a prolific scorer, he was also a wonderful all round player and he remains a legend not only for all Dundee supporters but also for supporters of Tottenham Hotspur, to whom he was transferred. Gilzean had everything; stunning ability to score from any distance, with both feet, something that is extremely rare nowadays. And of course, in the air, he was arguably the best header of a ball Scotland has ever known. He used to almost hang in the air before more often than not guiding his header into his opponents net. He will never be forgotten at Dens Park.

Back To The Race

The Dark Blues were hitting top form now and were only beaten twice in the run up to the Christmas and New Year period. They lay in a challenging position - only three points behind leaders Rangers. However, the New Year programme was a disaster and three defeats in a row at the hands of Rangers, Aberdeen and sadly, United, saw Dundee's Championship aspirations all but sunk for another season.

But there was still plenty of entertainment. Dundee's unpredictability was evident as the Scottish Cup draw was approaching and you just never knew which Dundee was going to turn up! When they did hit top form though, there were few teams that could live with them.

Goals were a plentiful and there were a few notable victories: 6-1 over St Johnstone and 6-0 over Third Lanark to name two. With the Scottish Cup just around the corner, the supporter's had high hopes that this would indeed be Dundee's year.

When the Cup draw was announced, Dundee were drawn against Forres Mechanics, a Highland league side and at first this was a bit of a relief....or was it?

Just before the game, memories, again, of past shockers against Berwick and Fraserburgh flashed into my mind. Surely not again, we would be okay with this one, I thought. And we were. Dundee didn't let us down. Despite the non-league side achieving much more than many top league sides by surprisingly scoring three times, the Dens men were never really in trouble and responded with six goals, taking them through to the next round.

This Dundee side seemed much more clinical than past sides and if teams scored three against them they just appeared to go up a gear and score more than the opposition.

January 11th 1964, Firs Park, Scottish League

East Stirling 1 - 5 Dundee

The 'Shire had won promotion the year before but were now finding life tough in the top Division. I was unable to play in my game at Sauchie because of an ankle injury, so as Dad couldn't make the game I went to Falkirk with my pal Tommy Millar instead.

And what a game it was! Dundee's opener came from the underrated Alan Cousin, the master of the double-shuffle. Gilzean then twice scored and a couple from Bobby Waddell - who was rapidly staking a claim for the starting spot - made up the tally. The pitch was covered in snow but, although sometimes in the past these conditions appeared to be a great leveller, Dundee seemed unaffected and turned on the style - much to the enjoyment of a healthy travelling support. The 'Shire just couldn't live with the pace and class of the Dark Blues and in the end the 5-1 score line was kind to the Stirlingshire side.

The Dens side just couldn't stop scoring - and not just in that game. In the 2nd round of the Scottish Cup, in front of a record home crowd of over 8,000 at Glebe Park, Brechin City were put to the sword as the Dark Blues hammered in nine (yes, *nine!)* goals to win 9-2. Then, in the League, Queen of the South were beaten 6-2. The goal machine was on full throttle with no sign of letting up. In round three of the cup, almost 18,000 turned out at Dens to see Forfar Athletic walloped 6-1! I wonder what the crowd would be today for a Dundee versus Forfar cup tie!

Dundee were flying. Dundee for the cup? Clearly it was not just me who thought that this was a distinct possibility as even the West of Scotland press appeared to be warming to this Dundee side. At home, I waited to hear the draw for the quarterfinals: Motherwell at Dens. We really could win this, I thought!

In the run up to the game, in the League Campaign, Hibs and Dunfermline were beaten 3-0 and 2-1. My hopes that this was really going to be Dundee's year were soaring, especially on the day when I heard that we had crushed St Mirren 9-2 at Dens! Dundee had been 4-0 ahead at half time in a game where the Dark Blues looked like scoring every time they came up the pitch. A hat-trick each for Gilzean and Waddell and singles from Cousin, Penman and Cameron, completed the rout. The 'Dee were really buzzing. Hampden here we come!

The Cup Runneth Over!

March 7th 1964, Dens Park

Scottish Cup Quarter Final

Dundee 1 - 1 Motherwell

On the day of the Scottish Cup tie against Motherwell, I was playing at Sauchie juniors ground and scored twice. We won 3-1. My adrenalin was pumping, both from the game and the thought of Dundee hopefully going through to the Semi Final of the Scottish Cup. Immediately after the final whistle however, I learned on meeting my Dad that Dundee had lost a last second equaliser and so had to be content with a 1-1 draw. Kenny Cameron, who was emerging as a prolific goal scorer, had given Dundee the lead and it had looked like it was going be enough to see the team through to the semi final – until virtually the last kick of the ball. The highlights were featured on *ScotSport* and it definitely looked as if we should have won. I'm not being biased, honest!

March 11th 1964, Fir Park, Scottish Cup Replay

Motherwell 2 - 4 Dundee

As I was playing myself every week, it was still near impossible to see any of Dundee's matches so when we realised that we would have to play again, Dad and I decided very quickly that we would travel to Motherwell on the Wednesday evening to cheer on our team in the replay.

The road to Lanarkshire was absolutely nose-to-tail with supporter's buses and cars from Dundee. When we eventually arrived at the stadium, queues at the Dundee end were over thirty yards long and, when we finally got through the turnstiles, it was clear that we were going to have difficulty seeing the game at all. When the teams kicked off, such was the crowd, we could only see one half of the pitch and had to rely on the shouts of the crowd further down the terracing to let us know what was going on. At half time it was 1-1 - but we didn't even see the Dundee goal! From our position on the packed terracing, we could only see the faraway goalmouth. Great.

However, later, after the interval, with Dundee attacking the faraway end, we had a perfect view of Dundee's three second-half goals! With just over a quarter of an hour gone in the second period, Gilzean hit a rocket from more than twenty yards and when it flashed into the net the whole terracing erupted in a blaze of jumping dark blue and white. The atmosphere was like nothing I had ever seen before. But then Motherwell equalised - or so we were told, we didn't see the goal going in - which tempered the hopping about a little. However, Dundee were pressing and with twenty minutes left we went ahead with a Kenny Cameron counter. And around ten minutes later, Bobby Waddell scored again, making it 4-2. Then: the sound of the full-time whistle - bliss! Happiness personified!! On leaving the stadium, Dad and I were literally swept out of Fir Park. At one stage both my feet were off the ground as the massive Dundee support left the stadium. What a night! The crowd had been over 26,000 with an estimated 8,000 from Dundee but most notable of all, we were in the semi-finals!

What a contrast on the Saturday after though. We lost 3-1 to Airdrie at Broomfield in front of less than 1,000 fans! Unpredictable or what?!

On the following Monday at 60 Ochil Street, we listened in for the semi final draw. Rangers, Dunfermline and Kilmarnock were the other teams involved. Then it came through: Dundee v Kilmarnock. We were happy with that, although we knew it wouldn't be an easy one. Nowadays we hear commentators talking about the "new firm", a reference to United and Aberdeen emanating from the eighties, when both clubs had a purple patch in their club's histories. But in the early sixties a similar reference could have easily been made to Dundee and Kilmarnock or indeed Dunfermline, as these three clubs were regular challengers to the might of the "old firm".

The run up to the semi wasn't great. After we lost to Airdrie we went down 4-2 to Hearts, which ended a long, undefeated run. However, I was still reasonably confident that we could beat Kilmarnock at Ibrox and get to the Cup Final. Would my confidence be rewarded? That was the $64,000 question!

March 28th 1964, Ibrox Stadium

Scottish Cup Semi Final

Dundee 4 - 0 Kilmarnock

I was playing for Sauchie Juniors at Bonnybridge that day, but in a way, I wished I hadn't of been. Don't get me wrong, all I lived for was playing football but it's not every day that the team you support is playing for a place in the Cup Final! All during my game, in which I scored twice in a 5-2 win, flashes of how Dundee might be doing kept surging into my mind. It wasn't as if I wasn't concentrating on my own game - nothing would have deterred me from that - but the game at Ibrox just seemed to drift in and out of my subconscious! When our final whistle sounded I couldn't wait to hear the result. As I came off the field, Dad gave me the fantastic news, "4-0 Dundee!!" We were in the Final!

Dad and I listened to the car radio on the way home and learned that the Dark Blues had certainly hit top form! Goals from Gilzean (2), Penman and an O.G from Killie defender, McFadzean, saw them through to their first Scottish Cup Final since 1952! Dundee had led 1-0 at the interval but, after the break, Dundee's class shone and three further goals gave them an emphatic win. I expected Dundee to win, but a 4-0 score line absolutely encouraged me to think that the Scottish Cup was Dens Park bound. My confidence was sky high.

April 4th 1964, Dens Park

Dundee 2 - 1 Kilmarnock

My football season had finished rather early with a recurrence of an ankle problem, which forced me out of the last two fixtures - but that meant I could see two of the games in the build up to the cup final!

The first one against Kilmarnock was a tough one. Kilmarnock were looking to extract revenge for their recent semi final defeat - and they gave us a real test! Kenny Cameron had put us in front but "Killie" were always threatening. We lived dangerously for some time before the Ayrshire side finally equalised and it looked as if it would finish all square - but then came a dramatic last minute winner by Alan Gilzean. The big Dundee striker hammered home a stunning strike with only seconds left on the clock! Roll on Hampden, I thought!

April 18th 1964, Dens Park

Dundee 5 - 2 Partick Thistle

Dad couldn't make the game and so I elected to travel to Dens on my own. I was still only sixteen and not eligible to drive, so I made that old familiar journey of getting the bus and train.

I was at Dens Park by 2.00pm and took my place half way up the South Enclosure, exactly adjacent to the half way line. The sun was shining which added to the joy of waiting on the teams' arrival on the pitch, which was eventually greeted by a healthy 12,000 crowd.

It wasn't long before Dundee turned on the style and there was a bit of what would nowadays be termed as "showboating" as the Dark Blues played their studied, easy on the eye football - but with a cutting edge! Gilzean scored twice taking his tally to an incredible 50 for the season! Dundee's other goals came from Alex Stuart (2) and Andy Penman as they cantered to an easy win in their last home League fixture.

I joined in a standing ovation for the players as they left the pitch. I just felt so proud to be a Dundee fan. As I made my way down the steps to the exits, I left Dens Park convinced that by this time next week, Dundee would be Scottish Cup winners!

April 25th 1964, Hampden Park, Scottish Cup Final

Rangers 3 - 1 Dundee

Dad and I travelled by bus and train to Glasgow for the game as opposed to travelling by car, as Dad, with such a big crowd expected, wasn't too keen to leave his car near the stadium. As mentioned before, there was no segregation in these days so when we took our place in the stadium, we found ourselves standing underneath the old North Stand in the enclosure - surrounded by Rangers fans. Oops! There were, however, one or two Dundee voices around but the majority of the Dark Blues support had congregated behind the goals at the traditional "Celtic" end. There was a big Dundee support in the main stand as well. It was estimated that there were around 30,000 travelling Dundee fans in a crowd of over 120,000.

As the teams came out, the atmosphere was scary, almost like a gladiatorial contest in the Roman Colosseum. This, I thought, was what it was all about. I momentarily imagined myself out on the pitch. Was I nervous for them? You bet! I couldn't have been more so even if I *had* of been playing!

The game kicked off and shortly afterwards Dundee could have been ahead when Hugh Robertson saw a shot kicked off the line. Soon after, the Ibrox side took control and Dundee's 'keeper, Bert Slater, had to pull off some great heroic saves to keep us in the game.

In the second half, Rangers pressed for an opener and despite even more quite incredible saves from the courageous Dundee 'keeper, they took the lead with about 20 minutes to go. The Rangers fans around us almost shook the stadium, it was complete pandemonium - but nothing compared to what was to happen only seconds later.

Dundee restarted the game and only seconds later Alex Stuart's long ball found Kenny Cameron who seemed to turn and hook the ball all in one movement over the Rangers goalkeeper - and into the net! 1-1!!! Incredible stuff! Dad and I were going mad in our dark blue and white colours amongst the mass of light blue. The Dundee fans were in full voice - which for a few minutes, drowned out the Rangers hordes.

With less than two minutes to go, I turned to ask Dad if he would be able to make the replay. But - STOP PRESS!!! What had I just done? What had I just said, with confidence? I should have known better. Rangers scored. Then seconds later, to rub salt in our aching wounds, they scored again. Then: the full-time whistle. Gutted.

I was almost numb with shock and disappointment as we made our way out of Hampden Park. We had lost. We had *lost*. My numbness was also down to the unbelievable fact that we hadn't played to form. Bert Slater had been fantastic but the team never really performed like they could.

In later years, I spoke often about that game to Bert Slater and, like me, he was of the opinion that the real Dundee didn't turn up that day. I still believe to this day, that if Dundee had played to their true potential, we would have won.

So Rangers finished as Champions and Cup Winners but the consolation, to me anyway, was that the footballing Taysiders were the real entertainers that season. They had played some wonderful stuff and to finish the season empty handed was a major injustice.

They Think It's All Over - It Is Now

On the following Wednesday we met up with the Mortimers at Falkirk for Dundee's last league game of the season. Talk about an anti-climax! What a contrast from the red-hot atmosphere of the Cup Final. Before a crowd of only 3,000, Dundee, minus Gilzean and Cameron, cruised to a 2-0 victory, with Andy Penman scoring the two goals. The team played some nice football that night but I got the impression that they were just going through the motions and, at times, they seemed to be treating the game like a training session. However, winning comfortably was no consolation for what we had suffered in the previous week.

But despite the deep disappointment of losing in the Cup Final, I suppose it had been a fantastic season. We finished in sixth place, equal on points with Dunfermline in fifth, and only four points behind runners up Kilmarnock - but ten behind Champions Rangers. At various stages of the League competition, we had looked as if we could bring the Championship to Dens for the second time in three years. However, at vital times, we lacked the consistency necessary to sustain our challenge.

The football the team had played though had been at times outstanding and results such as 9-2 against St Mirren, 6-1 against St Johnstone at Perth, 4-0 against Hibs at Easter Road and 4-0 against Kilmarnock in the semi final of the Scottish Cup at Ibrox, was testimony to that. The club had finished the highest scorers in Scotland, with a massive 94 goals to their credit and normal service was resumed as we finished, again, higher than United in the table! It had been entertainment plus!

That season, a new Summer Cup was introduced in which, to be honest, I don't think anyone was interested, including the clubs themselves. The Old Firm declined to get involved and it was a tired and disinterested looking Dundee that took part, winning only one of their six games. Aberdeen beat Hibs 3-2 in the final but nobody seemed to care. Not me anyway! Roll on the next season.

Chapter 14

In Transition

Season 1964-65 would be different. Ok, there would still be European Football because by reaching the Cup Final we had qualified for the European Cup Winners Cup, but the difference was that the team that had brought the Championship to Dens, and had thrilled the whole of Europe with their stunning performances, was breaking up.

Ian Ure had joined Arsenal for £62,500 and Alan Gilzean, after refusing terms for the new season, was eventually transferred to Spurs for £72,000. Gordon Smith, approaching forty years of age, was released at his own request. Wing half, Bobby Wishart, moved on to Airdrie and the classy Bobby Seith, although starting in the first five matches, was used sparingly in the coming season and eventually took up a coaching position at Dens.

The season opened on a real downer with the team losing four of their first five matches in the League Cup - two of them to United, which made matters even worse. Shankly then turned the team upside down for the remaining League Cup fixture against Motherwell, and included five youngsters; one being sixteen-year old Jocky Scott. And it worked. Dundee won 6-0 and suddenly the 'Dee' looked the part once more and in quick succession Falkirk and Aberdeen were both beaten 3-1. Things were definitely heating up - and in more ways than one. At Brockville against Falkirk, Jocky Scott was coming out of his shell and showed the "other" side of his character when he was sent off following a clash with Irish International Sammy Wilson (who would himself eventually finish up at Dens Park). And next up was United at Tannadice!

September 12th 1964, Tannadice Park

Dundee United 1 - 4 Dundee

With no game for me that day, Dad and I travelled to Tannadice. The atmosphere was electric and the United support were already taunting us about making it three in a row. Soon after the game began, the taunts starting ringing true as the home side took the lead and my heart was in my boots.

However, Alan Cousin equalised for Dundee before half time with an absolutely stunning goal. Hugh Robertson on the left wing danced round his full back and crossed for Waddell who headed against the post, but then a United defender hoofed the ball clear - but only as far as the on rushing Cousin who chested the ball down and, on the drop, hit a glorious lob into the net from around twenty-five yards. What a goal! The half time whistle sounded shortly after and as the teams left the field it was the Dundee fans who were singing!

Then, the Dark Blues came back with a vengeance in the second half - and we had a great view, being in the shed end behind the goal that they were attacking. Andy Penman sped down the wing leaving three defenders in his wake before crossing an inch perfect ball - the quality of which his predecessor, Gordon Smith, would have been proud - to Bobby Waddell who powered home a flashing header into the net. I can still see it in my mind to this day. The cross, the header, *GOAL!!!!* The crowd, packed like sardines behind the goal, going mad. Ah, the good old days!! And sixteen year old Jocky Scott, who had so impressed in his debut against Motherwell, scored a double as Dundee ran out 4-1 winners! It couldn't get better than this - could it?

Revenge Is Sweet

September 19th 1964, Dens Park

Dundee 4 - 1 Rangers

Dundee versus Rangers games in the sixties were always feisty affairs and as often as not Dundee would turn over the Ibrox giants. Rangers were a good side and their team was sprinkled with good players, many of them Internationals, but they couldn't match Dundee for classy football. The Dark Blues in their change strip of all white, despite losing an early goal, gained revenge for their Cup Final defeat by turning in an absolutely stunning performance to crush the Ibrox side 4-1.

Rangers had gone in front early on but Alan Cousin equalised, then a cracker from Alex Stuart and two from Hugh Robertson was enough blood on the 'Dee's hands to give them a satisfying victory. Hugh Robertson's second goal and Dundee's fourth had been of stunning quality with the little winger jinking this way and that in an amazing sixty yard run which culminated in a terrific strike past a helpless Rangers 'keeper. That day, Dundee forgot about the likes of Ure and Gilzean etc. - if even just for a short time!

In typical Dundee fashion though, we were brought down to earth with another huge bump, suffering two defeats in a row to Motherwell and Clyde - hardly a great build up to our next game against Falkirk.

October 10th 1964, Brockville Park

Falkirk 4 - 2 Dundee

We travelled to the game with the Mortimers, not sure what to expect because historically Dundee were never at their best at Brockville. After an impressive first half though in which goals from

Stuart and Cameron saw the 'Dee in front, we appeared to be coasting to a 2-1 victory. However, late in the second half, somehow, we ended up losing *three* goals in the last *ten* minutes. We lost 4-2! How can that be?! We never even looked like losing! Victory was in our grasp. That day, Dundee absolutely proved that they could be unpredictable - even throughout a single game!

In the next two games we were beaten by Kilmarnock and Hearts but a 3-1 victory over Dunfermline at Dens raised our hopes for a visit to Celtic Park the following week.

November 14th 1964, Celtic Park

Celtic 0 - 2 Dundee

Just along the road at Rutherglen, I appeared as a trialist for Falkirk against Clyde at Shawfield Stadium. The weather was horrendous and the rain was torrential for the whole duration of the game. We drew 2-2.

Just over couple of miles away at Celtic Park, Dundee were playing Celtic. The weather was so bad that the floodlights failed and the teams had to come off the pitch. The game looked like it was going to be abandoned but somehow the floodlights became operational once more - but Celtic probably wished that they hadn't!

Dundee apparently adapted to the conditions better than their Glasgow rivals and goals from Andy Penman and Stevie Murray gave Dundee a 2-0 win. The first question I asked after coming out of the shower (and boy, did I need one!) was the score from Parkhead. "2-0 Dundee!" I heard someone shout. Yes!!! It raised my hopes of a win in the European Cup Winners Cup, which was on the following Wednesday.

November 18th 1964, Dens Park
European Cup Winners Cup
Dundee 2 - 2 Zarragoza

It was almost like old times as over 21,000 turned out to welcome the teams. Although there was no Gilzean in their ranks, Dundee took an early lead through Steve Murray but the Spanish side dominated, however, and went 2-1 ahead before the interval. In the second half though, encouraged by a vociferous support, the Dark Blues took the game to their Spanish opponents and, almost on full time, Doug Houston equalised! We were saved!

Adios Amigos

In the return leg in Spain, Dundee started well; Hugh Robertson put Dundee ahead. But then the Dark Blues struggled to maintain a grip on the game. Bobby Cox was badly injured and although the Dens skipper tried to carry on, limping on the wing, he was no more than nuisance value and the Spanish side eventually overcame Dundee's stout defending to score twice and win 2-1. Dundee were out.

That defeat was tough to take but I had to be realistic; Dundee were in transition and there was no doubt they had missed the quality of the likes of Gilzean and Ure.

End Of A Beautiful Era

In between the two European ties, Dundee saw any chance of even a domestic challenge disappear. They drew three games consecutively against Partick Thistle, Hibs and St Johnstone. Gilzean - although unable to appear in Europe - had been operating on weekly contracts and against St Johnstone, in his last game in Dundee colours, he signed off in style by scoring a hat-trick. Around ten days later, the big striker was on his way to Tottenham Hotspur for £72,500. It was a sad day but he would forever live on in the hearts and minds of all Dundee supporters who were fortunate enough to see him strut his stuff in the Dark Blue of Dundee.

A Smart Little Cookie

Bob Shankly moved swiftly however to appease the fans that were hurting from the Gilzean transfer; he swooped to sign Charlie Cooke from Aberdeen for £40,000. Moving to Dundee from Aberdeen in those days was a step up for the talented midfielder and in a very short period of time he became a fan's favourite. His arrival was heralded with a 4-0 win over Airdrie. In later years, when I was training full time for a spell at Dens, I saw Charlie's skills at close quarters. What a marvellous player. A typical old-fashioned Scottish type player with the skills of a Brazilian International! Cooke would beat a man on a sixpence and turn about and do it again just for the fun of it!

With this type of skill at our disposal, we were hopeful of a Scottish Cup run and only one defeat in the next six games raised hopes of another Hampden final in April.

February 6th 1965, Muirton Park

Scottish Cup 1st Round

St. Johnstone 1 - 0 Dundee

Dundee took a huge support to Perth but unfortunately, even with some boisterous backing from the terraces, it didn't seem to make a difference. Before a crowd of 17,000, Dundee went down and out 1-0. After hearing the result I was devastated. Since 1961, I had been used to seeing and hearing of nothing but relative success for Dundee and now the season was, even at this early stage, all but over. Okay, we had lost some really good players but there seemed to me to be something wrong somewhere at Dens and this, I think, was confirmed a couple of weeks later when Bob Shankly resigned and became manager of Hibs.

Shanks For The Memories

I worked with Bob Shankly for twelve years at Stirling Albion where he was general manager. I remember as a youngster of thirteen when I was invited to train at Dens Park, being in awe of the man, and when I met him again at the age of twenty-six, my feelings had not changed. "Shanks" was as honest as the day was long. He called a spade a spade and if you didn't like what was being said, then that was tough. He was a lover of the game being played simply and whenever someone started to talk all the technical jargon - that is part and parcel of the game today - "Shanks" would reply that it was wrong to make a simple thing difficult.

I remember well, Davie Wilson, ex Rangers, then manager of Dumbarton, waxing lyrical to "Shanks" and Stirling Albion manager, Alex Smith, about the great "third running" of a German midfield player, to which "Shanks" replied, "Davie, I've been in the game for over forty years and I dinnae ken what ye're f*****n talkin' about!"

Also, after Dundee had defeated Cologne 8-1 in the European Cup, reputedly, when asked by a reporter what his tactics for the game had been, his reply was a classic. “Keep it simple, work harder than the opposition, pass the ball better and don’t just roll your sleeves up to here (pointing at his elbow), roll them up to here (pointing at his shoulder)!” Somehow I can’t imagine Arsene Wenger giving a similar response!!

Shanks was a real character and one day at Annfield, Stirling Albion’s old ground, the Queen, who had been visiting Stirling, was scheduled to meet the Guides and Scouts of Stirling in some sort of presentation, which was to take place at Annfield. Over 10,000 people thronged the terraces and when the Queen was introduced to Bob Shankly, Shanks was heard saying, “I wish you could come here every second Saturday.” The Albion were only drawing around 1,200 at their home matches! Bob Shankly - a legend.

Shankly’s successor was Bobby Ancell, the then manager of Motherwell. I never saw Ancell play but my Dad did and by all accounts he was a cultured full back. It was good also that under Ancell it was anticipated that the team should continue to play good passing football. We would wait and see, we thought.

February 27th 1965, Tynecastle Park

Scottish League Championship

Hearts 1 - 7 Dundee

Dundee visited Tynecastle to play Championship pace setters, Hearts. In the lead up to the game, Dundee had beaten Falkirk and won away at Kilmarnock - never an easy place to get a result. However, the 'Dee then lost to "bogey" team Clyde, dipping our confidence once again and, to make matters worse, Hearts had been undefeated at home for *two* years!

But there was loads of talent in this Dundee side. Under Ancell, the team continued to play the passing man to man football which had been the club's trademark and, that day, a Charlie Cooke inspired performance saw Dundee demolish the Tynecastle side 7-1! A shock to the system for the Hearts fans and players! Andy Penman and Kenny Cameron both recorded hat-tricks, with Alan Cousin netting a single. Alan actually scored at both ends - scoring an own goal late in the match! We forgave him for that though, considering the score!

I was playing a home game that day at Sauchie and we lost 2-0. I realised that something special had happened with Dundee however, as Dad had a grin on his face like a Cheshire Cat when greeting me on my exit from the dressing room. "7-1 Dundee!" was all he said.

The match was on the television that night! What a red letter day that was! I would have been happy to watch that TV coverage over and over again. In a strange way though, this performance only increased my frustration because Dundee's potential was there for all to see, but it was their inconsistency that was the problem - a problem that seemed difficult to overcome. Just how could a team that could take seven goals off the league leaders not actually be themselves challenging for the title! Oh dear, the joys of being a Dark Blue!!

Hearts were eventually "pipped" on goal average to the title on the last day of the season by Kilmarnock. If they had lost only 6-1 instead of 7-1 against Dundee, they would have taken the title!

March 20th 1965, Dens Park

Dundee 3 - 3 Celtic

Despite receiving treatment for a knee injury, I was deemed unfit for my game on the Saturday so as a "consolation", I travelled to Dens with Dad and my pal, Liam.

The game turned out to be a classic. Before a crowd of 18,000, two goals from Kenny Cameron and an own goal from Murdoch gave Dundee a share of the points, in a game that we really should have won. Celtic had their noses in front for most of the game but Dundee kept coming back, and when the third goal went in it set off pandemonium in the South Enclosure! Actually my pal was a Celtic fan and he was not a happy bunny! But did I care? Not a jot!

And so the League Campaign drifted on until it finished with a 2-2 draw at Airdrie in the final game of the season.

Summer Lovin' – Well, Not Quite

The Football authorities experiment of playing a Summer Cup, in which the "old firm" took no part, was again played out but Dundee, at any rate, again, appeared not to be interested - they lost four of their six games, two of them to United.

May 19th 1965, Muirton Park, Summer Cup

St Johnstone 2 - 3 Dundee

However, we made our way to Perth for Dundee's very last Summer Cup and competitive game of the season. Two goals from Kenny Cameron and an own goal from Richmond ensured that we finished with a win, which is always nice to go out on. The attendance was only 2,000 and our minds drifted back to the events of just over three years ago, when 26,500 fans packed this very same stadium to see Dundee confirmed as Scottish Champions. It all seemed so very far away now.

The season came to an end with little to excite the fans for the future. If we included the Forfarshire cup, in the seven games we played against United, we won only once against them. At Muirton, in the Summer Cup game, we had to endure taunts from the Saint's fans that, "United were kings on Tayside now!" Painful.

Although it was a worrying trend, we had to get things into perspective though. The reality was that we again finished in sixth place (not too bad) in the league, above United (definitely not too bad!) for the third time in four seasons. We ended four points behind fifth placed Rangers too - but ten behind Champions Killie. Our appetites were whetted.

Chapter 15

Nearly A Dream Come True

August 1965. I am invited by Bobby Ancell to spend two weeks full time training at Dens Park! Dundee had been monitoring my progress since I was thirteen, and when I got the call that they wanted to take a closer look, I was really excited - understatement!

When I arrived at the ground I was met by a man called Chris Squires, my landlord for the next two weeks, and another football hopeful, Bobby Rough. Chris drove us to what would be our home for the fortnight: 29 Cleghorn Street.

Chris and his wife were really homely people, and although the tenement flat was far from luxurious, it was comfortable enough. When Bobby and I were shown our quarters however, we instantly, and horrifyingly noted that there was just one double bed! Can't imagine budding young players today relishing that situation too much - and I have to say neither Bobby or myself were overjoyed about it either!

The fortnight was a dream come true for me, training and playing with and against my Dundee heroes; Charlie Cooke, Bobby Cox and Alex Hamilton, not to mention Alan Cousin (who had been my coach at Alloa Y.M.). At the end of the fortnight, I was asked to come back and play a trial. They would notify me. Later, I read in the National Press that they had signed Bobby Rough. Bobby went on to play a few times for the first team and I later met up with him at Stirling Albion. I was disappointed that I wasn't asked to sign there and then as I honestly felt that I had impressed, with respect, more than Bobby in my two weeks at the club.

Bobby Ancell was extremely nice to me as was Bobby Seith, who was now coaching at Dens, and they both ensured me, however, that they were seriously interested in my football future but just wanted to see me in action in a reserve match.

After the two weeks training were over, I was transferred to Bo'ness United from Sauchie. Bo'ness was, in junior terms, a big club and I hoped that it would be the catalyst that would see me land at Dens Park, not as a supporter - but as a player.

August 14th 1965, Fir Park

Motherwell 1 - 0 Dundee

Dad and I travelled to Fir Park for the first League Cup game of the season and, as we made our way to the stand, Bobby Ancell came out of the player's entrance and immediately recognised me. He said, "Stay where you are for a minute." He vanished inside and came out with two centre stand tickets for Dad and me, adding, "I want to look after this young man," to Dad. It is an understatement to say that Dad was chuffed to bits... and so was I!

However, our joy was short lived as Motherwell won 1-0.

August 18th 1965, Dens Park, League Cup

Dundee 0 - 0 Dundee United

As Dad was working, I travelled to the game with my pal, Liam. We stood high up at the Provost Road end amongst a crowd of around 25,000; the atmosphere was tense. It ended up, however, not actually being a great game - typical Derby stuff. End to end play with Dundee always looking the better side but unfortunately they were unable to convert their outfield superiority into goals. Dundee employed a 4-2-4 system and defensively they looked sound but seemed to lack the vital spark necessary to win the match.

Snap!

August 21st 1965:

Celtic Park

Celtic 0 - 2 Dundee

&

Newtown Park

Bo'ness United 2 - 0 West Calder

The following Saturday, Dundee visited Celtic Park, the same day that I was making my Bo'ness debut. Two goals from Kenny Cameron ensured a Dundee win of 2-0 and at Bo'ness I scored twice in a 2-0 debut win! I was delighted when I heard the score from Parkhead, a double whammy for me!

August 25th 1965, Shawfield Stadium

Championship League

Clyde 0 - 2 Dundee

Here, we witnessed a comfortable 2-0 win for the Dark Blues with Penman and new signing Carl Bertelsen notching the goals. Bertelsen had been signed from Morton in the close season and had sparkled in the pre-season friendlies (later, however, the goals would dry up for the Danish born forward and he would be under pressure to retain a starting place). That day, Dundee looked good and confident and it was interesting for me to watch as I recognised some of the moves that had been worked on whilst I was training full time at Dens.

However, just when it seemed certain that we were going to qualify for the group stages, we did our usual and on the following Saturday we lost to Motherwell at Dens. This meant that to give ourselves a chance of qualifying for the next stage of the competition, we absolutely had to win the return derby at Tannadice the following Wednesday.

September 1st 1965, Tannadice Park

Dundee United 1 - 3 Dundee

We had only beaten United once in the last eight meetings but the "bogey" was to be burst this night. Dundee had gone into a 2-0 lead in the first half, in what was a tense derby atmosphere. The game didn't follow what had been, of late, the usual derby pattern with Dundee doing the attacking and United breaking away to score. No, this time it was the other way round. United had the lion's share of the game but it was the Dark Blues who demonstrated the cutting edge and, two goals up towards half time, they started to look more confident and ended the half well in command.

United then scored with around half an hour to go in the second half, which delved us into nail biting stuff. But the 'Dee weathered the storm and scored a clinching third ten minutes later for a deserved victory. Two goals from Kenny Cameron and a rare strike from Steve Murray clinched the points. It was a good display from Dundee - and a win against United was well overdue!

In the final game in the League Cup section, Dundee needed to win against Celtic at Dens. However, before 28,000, the Glasgow side triumphed by 3-1 - we were out of the League Cup. I was a bit sick that we didn't qualify but realised only a few days later what "feeling sick" actually felt like!

September 11th 1965, Dens Park

Dundee 0 - 5 Dundee United

On my home front, the following week, I scored twice in my game against Camelon - we won 8-0! However, my celebratory mood was soon extinguished when I learned that the 'Dee had been dumped 5-0 nil by United at Dens. Devastated. Sure glad I missed that one! At Dens, United had been much more physical than Dundee and had won easily against a dark blue side who were far too "tippy tappy". Strangely, Dundee had had a lot of the ball but were too easily pushed out of the way by United who, in the end, won as comfortably as the score suggests. It took me a few days to get that one out of my system!

The next few games were a mixed bag. The Dark Blues recovered from the devastating defeat from United by winning 3-2 at Pittodrie against Aberdeen. Then followed a 1-1 draw against Rangers before 24,000 at Dens, with Dane Carl Bertelson scoring our goal. Next, a 0-0 draw with Hearts, a 2-0 win against Falkirk, and finally it was a 5-3 defeat at Kilmarnock that set the tone for the next match against United at Dens. Hopefully we would make up for what we suffered the last time.

October 23rd 1965, Dens Park, Forfarshire Cup

Dundee 1 - 0 Dundee United

It might only have been a Forfarshire cup game but, in these days, that tournament wasn't taken lightly. As I had no game that day, I telephoned Chris Squires, with whom I had stayed during my spell training full time at Dens, to see if he could get me a ticket for the game. When I telephoned him the next evening to see if he had been successful, he told me that Mr Ancell, Dundee's manager, had indicated that I was to come to the player's entrance and that someone would look after me from there. Great! So, on the day of the match, I took my place in the stadium along with some of the reserve players as an invited guest, and in a crowd of over 14,000, watched Kenny Cameron notch the winner for the 'Dee. The goal came in the second half and it was richly deserved. It wasn't a great goal but any goal against United was deemed as impressive and, as far as I was concerned, it was sweet revenge for the hammering we had received only a month or so earlier. Okay, it was hardly a beating like we had received from United but it was still a win, and the fact that we played much the better football pleased me immensely!

Only The Dark Blues Will Do

At Bo'ness United, I was flying. Liverpool had been monitoring my progress and I was invited down to "The Reds" for a week as a trialist. I played in a Merseyside derby, albeit that it was a reserve game but we lost 3-0 to a strong Everton side. Still, not many can say that they have played in a Merseyside derby! According to the National Press, Aston Villa, Hearts, Falkirk, Partick Thistle, Manchester City, Hibs, and Hearts were all monitoring my progress. I was thrilled! But I was waiting for the phone call from Dundee.

After the win against United, there was a 2-1 reverse to Celtic, but then followed a four game unbeaten run; St Mirren, Hibs, St Johnstone were all beaten and a draw was gained at Morton - so our confidence was running high going into our next game.

November 27th 1965, Annfield Park

Stirling Albion 1 - 4 Dundee

A severe early frost took its toll on Junior Football and my game was cancelled but it was great for me that the cancellation coincided with Dundee's visit to Stirling and so Dad and I made our way to Annfield Park, where we met up with the Mortimers. The underfoot conditions at Annfield weren't great and the pitch seemed to be pretty frosty. Some Dundee players looked to be wearing trainers rather than boots but Dundee didn't seem to be affected as we watched a super performance! Goals from Cameron, Penman, Houston and Murray gave Dundee the points in a 4-1 win. To be honest, Dundee cantered through the match and could have won by even more. An early goal from Kenny Cameron seemed to settle the Dark Blues and after the second goal from Andy Penman went in it was a case of, how many more? 4-1 was really kind to the Albion but, as I watched from the Albion terracing, little did I know what was about to unfold the following week.

The next week, my manager at Bo'ness advised me that Stirling Albion wanted me to turn out as a trialist - against Dundee United at Tannanadice. I wasn't too keen as I had no interest in joining the Albion but after some discussion with my Dad, I decided to play. It was at least a chance to put one over on United, I thought!

As I ran out at Tannadice, I looked up to the very spot where I stood cheering on the Dark Blues, at the traditional "shed" end. Wouldn't it be nice if I could score at that end tonight, I thought to myself!

We however lost 2-1 (unfortunately it wasn't me who stuck our only goal in the net!) but I played really well and gave United plenty of problems! After the game, Sammy Baird, Albion's manager, ushered me into the Tannadice manager's office. He sat me down and asked me to sign, promising that I would be his first choice right winger - but I refused the terms. I wanted to go to Dundee.

The *Daily Express* carried a back page story the next day, saying that the Albion wanted to sign me. Bobby Seith, the Dundee coach, then talked to my Dad on the telephone and within days I received a letter from Mr Ancell inviting me to play for Dundee reserves at Dens the following Saturday. However, the date coincided with an important fixture for Bo'ness and the club refused Dundee permission to play me. I was so frustrated! Later, that frustration turned to anger. Bo'ness was always reluctant to let players go on a Saturday (my game for Albion was on a Wednesday evening which didn't clash with a Bo'ness fixture), and as another opportunity to play with Dundee never arose, the chance to sign for my boyhood heroes was gone. Words cannot describe, even to this day, the pain of that realisation.

What A Difference A Day Makes

After several visits to my home by the Albion manager, Sammy Baird, I decided to then sign for Stirling Albion. Only *24 hours* later, however, I was devastated to learn that Manchester City had tabled an offer for me at the very time that I was signing on the dotted line for Albion. I was distraught. What a difference a day makes. Twenty.

Four. Little. Hours. Training with International players on a full time basis would have improved me as a player and, to be honest, I never really got over it.

The next time I would see Dundee was when I was playing against them in a reserve match, which we won 5-1 at Annfield. I headed a goal past Dundee keeper, John Arrol. Our centre forward, Willie Traynor, crossed from the left and I managed to get my head to the ball before a Dundee defender, to score. I remember it well because although I was a regular scorer, it was the only time that I had ever scored with my head! (I also scored the winner against them in a game the following season) It seemed strange, playing against Dundee. Since I had been a wee boy, every time I had seen Dundee in the flesh, so to speak, I had been rooting for them to win but here I was doing my best to ensure they would be beaten! In the game when I scored the winning goal, I remember that Dundee had played a really strong reserve team.

From memory, the Dundee team that day was as follows: Donaldson, Hamilton and Swan. Selway, Easton and Houston. Penman, a.n. other, Duncan, a.n other, and I think it was Cameron. I was directly against “Hammy”, who remembered me from my time at Dens and taunted me the whole game. I had the last laugh however when I scored the winner! It probably looked a simple tap in from around six yards but with “Hammy” covering the near post and goalkeeper Ally Donaldson stretching himself out, there actually wasn't a lot of space for me to put the ball in the net, so I had to guide it between the two of them. Strangely, the only emotion that I felt was joy at scoring. That I had scored the winner against the team that I supported really didn't enter into my mind. It runs in my mind that it was Andy Penman's last game in a Dark Blue jersey and I played against him the next week also when he turned out for Rangers at Ibrox.

For the next couple of seasons however, I never got the chance to see my beloved Dark Blues in action but the first question on my lips after all my games was always, "How did Dundee get on?"

Untimely And Unfair

My playing career turned out to be a short one however, as I contracted a serious illness, TB. I fought against it with all my might, but a couple of years later I finally had to succumb to the fact that I just wasn't well enough to play. My playing career had turned into a nightmare and, although it had all started so promisingly, it was now in tatters. I knew deep down that something was wrong because my biggest asset was my pace and I felt, as time went on, that I was becoming weaker and towards the end, well frankly, I just couldn't run at all. I had to give up playing and then spent four weeks in hospital and the next six months unable to work. I temporarily lost interest in the beautiful game.

During the time that I was ill I saw very few games and indeed, as mentioned above, fell out of love with football in general. However, I did go to the League Cup final in 1967 when Dundee ran Celtic close in a classic of a game only to lose 5-3. I wasn't too well on the day of the game but I was determined to go as it was an opportunity to see Dundee win a trophy at Hampden Park.

Strangely, my strongest memory of that game was that we went a goal down just as I was taking my seat. We fought back well though and I can remember, at 4-3, thinking that we could get something from the game. But it was not to be and a late Celtic goal sealed our fate.

May 1st 1968, Dens Park

Fairs Cup, Semi Final

Dundee 1 - 1 Leeds Utd

Later that season, I managed to get to Dens Park for the Semi Final of the Fairs Cup (now the UEFA cup). It was against Leeds United and the atmosphere was like old times as 25,000 fans turned out to roar the teams on. Dad and I stood in the stand enclosure that night and watched Dundee really give the star studded English side a run for their money. The Dark Blues started really well but Leeds were dangerous on the break and opened the scoring after twenty five minutes. This reverse signalled a spell of Dundee pressure and there were a couple of close things in and around the Leed's goalmouth as Dundee turned up the heat. Jackie Charlton in the Leeds defence looked immense and he had to be, as the Dark Blues forced the pace. Then, around eight minutes before half time, the ground erupted when Bobby Wilson equalised with a well-placed header.

The second half was at times frantic but Dundee couldn't get the goal that would have given them an advantage to take to Elland Road for the second leg.

In the second leg Dundee did what few English and Continental teams had done that season i.e. give Leeds a decent game, and although we lost the second leg 1-0, we left with our heads held high. Leeds United were tearing apart almost everything in front of them and to run the English giants so close was, in itself, a victory of sorts.

So Many Cups, Not One Of Them Ours

February 21st 1970, Bayview Park

Scottish Cup, Quarter Final

East Fife 0 - 1 Dundee

In 1970, I travelled with Dad through to Methil for the Quarter Final tie of the Scottish Cup against East Fife and took my place in a 15,000 crowd (yes, 15,000!). A goal from Alex Bryce gave Dundee a 1-0 win that afternoon and that certainly made me feel a bit better! Pat Quinn, who had played for Scotland whilst with Motherwell, may have been in the twilight of his career, but the wily little mid-fielder caused a lot of problems that day in the black and gold of East Fife. Although Dundee had been the better side, a Quinn inspired East Fife had not lacked effort and I was mighty glad to hear the final whistle. We drew Celtic in the semi again but this time went down 2-1, in front of 64,000 at Hampden. A sixth placed finish saw us finish two points behind United.

In season 1970-71 Dundee qualified for what was called the Texaco Cup. This was a competition that involved both Scottish and English teams. Dundee were drawn against Wolverhampton Wanderers, then of the First Division in England, which was the top tier at that time.

In the first leg at Dens, although Wallace scored, Wolves always looked physically stronger and we went down 2-1. Although Dundee had a lot of the ball, they really never got behind the Wolves' defence often enough to cause the English side any real concern. The general consensus of opinion of those around us in the main stand was that Dundee had been unlucky but, looking at it from a professional perspective, I couldn't agree with that point of view. We lost the second leg 1-0.

So, from 1968-69 to 1970-71, the games I saw were few and far between but I still followed the team from afar though and listened for their results. However, this was a time that I needed to get my own life in order.

On the 13th February 1971, I was married to Elma Graham, my girlfriend of four years. Dundee were playing Stirling Albion in the Scottish Cup at Dens that day and won 2-0. How did I know that they had won? Well, I must confess that I sneaked away from the main reception area in the hotel to find out the result from one of the waiters. Got to get my priorities right!

As the season wore on, it was Elma who encouraged me back to following my team in person again - every week. I was back working now and studying hard for my diploma in Remedial Massage and Manipulation (later I would qualify in Sports and Fitness Therapy also) and Saturdays were beginning to be something to look forward to again. At Dens, there were real signs that Dundee were coming good again and under John Prentice the Dark Blues were once again turning on the football style.

Chapter 16

Where's My Scarf?

I started season 1972-73 as a professional player but it was the season before, 1971-72, that I had completely rekindled my enthusiasm for football. I had started doing a bit of training in the hope that I could perhaps one day play again at senior level and I also decided that I would see as many games as possible. So I decided to seek out the blue and white scarf that had been mothballed for all but a few occasions in the last few seasons.

August 14th 1971, Pittodrie Stadium, League Cup

Aberdeen 1 - 1 Dundee

Dundee's League Cup section included Falkirk, Clyde and Aberdeen - who we were drawn to play away on the opening day - and the 'Dee could not have been given a harder task.

The previous season, Aberdeen had finished runners up in the League to Celtic and were tipped to challenge strongly again this season. So, Dad and I had decided to make the long trip up North to Aberdeen on what was a gloriously sunny afternoon. We took our seats in the main stand towards the beach end of the ground, and in a crowd of around 20,000, there was a good following from Tayside.

John Duncan gave Dundee the lead in the first half but it was at the opposite end of the ground to that where we were sitting, so we couldn't really see what happened. But I do remember Duncan's shot and the reaction of the Dundee supporters around us - wild! Then, Mike Hewitt in the Dundee goal was magnificent as he defied everything that the Dons threw at him, before, however, conceding a late equaliser.

Aberdeen had been impressive and had pressed for much of the game but Dundee had stood firm and in the first half had shown that, in John Duncan, they had a striker who could turn half chances into goals. Mike Hewitt in goal had one of these games that goalkeepers dream about - defying the Dons time after time.

On leaving the stadium, a disgruntled Aberdeen fan had turned to a Dundee supporter saying, "Yer goalie saved ye." The Dundee fan's answer was a classic.

"Yeah," he replied, "And he's just our reserve 'keeper, good job we never played our first team goalie!"

August 25th 1971, Brockville Park

Falkirk 1 - 0 Dundee

A 2-2 draw at home to Falkirk and a 1-0 win away at Clyde was the build up to Dundee's visit to Brockville. Dad couldn't make it so I travelled to Falkirk with James Mortimer - but we were really awful and lost 1-0. In more recent times Dundee had done quite well at Brockville but this was a truly abysmal game. The Dark Blues never really played anything like to form and although the score line was close, in reality, we never really looked like saving even a point. The joys of following the 'Dee!

Me Plus One

August 28th 1971, Dens Park

Dundee 3 - 1 Aberdeen

As told earlier, I had been recently married to Elma, and now I was trying to get *her* interested in going to the football with me. I eventually persuaded her to exchange her "shopping day" to go with me to Dens for the visit of the Dons. I was so glad Elma came to this game as it was like I was showing off my baby and was bursting with pride!

Aberdeen brought a good loud following south from the Granite City; Elma and I seemed to be surrounded by them! The Dundee fans were noisy as well and, before a crowd of over 13,000, we saw an excellent Dundee performance. Goals from Gordon Wallace (2) and a single from Doug Houston gave us a 3-1 win. Unfortunately however, it wasn't enough for us to qualify for the next stage of the League Cup as Falkirk pipped us by a point. Elma enjoyed the match though and she accompanied me on several occasions in the future - but still mostly stuck to the shopping. Like most women, she didn't understand the offside rule! (Shouldn't have written that - my daughter will have my guts for garters for saying such a thing!!)

Back To Business

The League Campaign started at Aberdeen and we were beaten 3-0, however, all I could think about was the next game against Dundee United at Dens Park.

September 11th 1971, Dens Park

Dundee 6 - 4 Dundee United

We had been having the proverbial nightmare against our neighbours from across the road and had lost the last *seven* derbies. So Dad, the Mortimers, and I travelled to Dens with some trepidation.

The South enclosure was full so we stood further along the terracing, towards the Provost Road end. It was a magnificently sunny day and as the teams took to the field, with Dundee now sporting white shirts and blue pants as their first choice strip and United in all Tangerine, the respective supports roared - ready for battle!

The game initially took the usual derby format that we had been used to: Dundee doing all the attacking but having no luck. Then what was the norm in the recent run of non-success against United happened; the "Arabs" broke away and scored. 0-1 and a look of déjà vu came across all our faces.

However, this surely couldn't last, we thought. Dundee were playing really well. Alex Bryce was outstanding and the Dark Blues were dominating the game, with United hanging on to their lead - with more than a slice of good fortune. Surely, we thought, a goal had to come. Then, the "gods" must have heard us. Bryce equalised! And then, with the crowd still on their feet cheering, he scored again to make it 2-1 before half time! My adrenaline was pumping!

And the second half was a cracker! The white shirted 'Dee took United apart. Goals from Wallace and two from Jocky Scott made it 5-1! Jocky Scott's goal was a classic as he wrong footed three United defenders and almost nonchalantly rolled the ball into the United net. We were absolutely loving it - and there was still twenty-five minutes to go! Pile them on! Bryce was dictating the play and Wallace and Scott were giving United a torrid time. Every time we were up the pitch we looked like scoring. "C,mon Dundee, rub it in!" We had all been waiting for this moment, telling ourselves after every United defeat that, one day, we would give them a real hammering.

United then scored to make it 5-2 but only minutes later, Dundee hit back and went up the pitch to score again! At that stage, Dundee were toying with their city rivals! However, with about ten minutes left, ex 'Dee, Kenny Cameron, now of course with United, scored to make it 6-3. And two minutes later he scored again to make it 6-4! Surely not, we thought!! Please no! We started to feel just a little uncomfortable. Thankfully, however, there were no more scares and we saw the match out comfortably enough. Phew. Why is that you can never get an easy game when supporting the 'Dee!

There is no doubt that these two late goals took the shine off, what had been at times, a devastating Dundee performance. The result made it look respectable for United and, amazingly, it was *their* fans that left the stadium singing. We had the chance to record the defeat of all defeats over our closest rivals but, in typical Dundee fashion, we blew it. On reflection, however, after the game, going home in the car, we concurred that United had been outclassed in a superb Dundee performance. It was, for eighty minutes or so, a performance to savour, and the feeling we had when that fifth goal went in to make it 5-1 with twenty-five minutes left, was almost indescribable. We genuinely thought that seven or eight was on the cards. This Dundee side, though, looked to be the best that I had seen since the halcyon days of the early sixties.

September 15th 1971, Dens Park, UEFA Cup

Dundee 4 - 2 AB Copenhagen

In the UEFA cup Dundee had been drawn with AB Copenhagen of Denmark, and on the Wednesday following the triumph over United, we travelled to Dens for the first leg.

Alex Bryce was again in fine form and added to his double against United by weighing in with another brace, and further goals from Wallace and an emerging youngster, Duncan Lambie, gave Dundee a comfortable win of 4-2. The Danes were a big physical looking team but to be honest, they didn't really cause us many problems.

I left, however, feeling that we should have scored more. It was a little worrying and I hoped that we wouldn't regret the fact that we seemed to take our foot off the gas and content ourselves with a two goal margin to take into the second leg in Denmark.

September 18th 1971, Bayview Park

East Fife 2 - 5 Dundee

Next up was East Fife in the League and, at a well-filled Bayview, we watched a truly outstanding Dundee performance. The football the team was playing was easy on the eye and the front three of Wallace, Scott and Duncan, struck fear into the opposition. Duncan seemed to have a roving commission, sometimes on the right wing but nearly always on the end of crosses, from either side. It was little wonder that he was nicknamed "Gillie" as he was the nearest thing to Gilzean that we had seen since the sixties.

When Jocky was in the mood he could destroy defences on his own. And Gordon Wallace, although he was never the quickest, was quicker than most when it counted - in the penalty box. Gordon worked so hard, never giving defences a minute's peace and was terrific at linking play - a real team player.

An amazing goal spree by Gordon, who netted four times, and a scorcher of a goal by left back Davie Johnstone, saw Dundee depart Methil with a 5-2 win.

Although there had been some depressing times in the late sixties when the Championship side had broken up, from the time that I had started supporting the club in 1954, Dundee had always been looked upon as one of the "big six". Rangers, Celtic, Hearts, Hibs, Aberdeen and Dundee were the big city clubs and Dundee were, during this time, always looked on as one of the country's best footballing sides, albeit sometimes lacking the killer touch. This team however, was showing signs that not only could they play classy football but that they could find the net as well.

I have to say that following the team on a regular basis in these days was a real pleasure. Okay, from time to time they would still let you down - it would not have been Dundee if they hadn't - but the football the team played was, on occasion, worth the admission money itself.

(Probably - along with the fact that United are in the SPL whilst we are currently a league below in the First Division - the biggest negative I find in following the team week in and week out today, season 2009-2010, is that the football we play doesn't, at the moment, anywhere near compare with the great teams of the past. That was always my consolation in defeat. "Okay, so sometimes we lose, but Dundee played the football!" Sadly this is no longer always the case. It is a different financial ball game now. However, considering that we almost went out of business a few seasons ago, the club has done remarkably well and with Jocky Scott back at the helm and an ambitious board, I have high hopes that soon we will be plying our trade again where we belong: in the SPL)

September 29th 1971, Gladsaxe Stadium

UEFA Cup, 1st Round, 2nd leg

AB Copenhagen 0 - 1 Dundee

In the second leg of the EUFA tie with AB Copenhagen, a John Duncan goal gave us a 1-0 win and a 5-2 aggregate victory. My fears that we might live to regret not scoring more in the first leg at Dens were forgotten. Dundee coasted through the game and perhaps might have won by more.

October 20th 1971, Müngersdorfer Stadium

UEFA Cup, 2nd Round, 1st Leg

Cologne 2 - 1 Dundee

Memories were jogged when it was announced that Dundee had drawn Cologne in the second round of the EUFA Cup, as Cologne of course had been European Cup rivals in 1962.

In the first leg in Germany, Dundee, according to press reports, had started well before going behind to a disputed goal. Then, the underrated Alex Kinninmonth equalised but the German side went on to clinch a first leg lead, scoring a late goal. However, Kinninmonth's counter had kept our hopes alive for the second leg at Dens Park in a fortnight's time.

In the lead up to the second leg we had drawn at home against Partick Thistle but recorded a fine 3-1 away victory against a decent Motherwell side at Fir Park.

November 3rd 1971, Dens Park, UEFA Cup, 2nd Leg

Dundee 4 - 2 Cologne

Dad and I travelled to the match along with my Father-in-law, Alex. The south enclosure was standing only in these days and so we took our place half way up, adjacent to the half way line, in a packed terracing; what an atmosphere!

After less than quarter of an hour, we went ahead on the night, equalising on aggregate. John Duncan rose majestically in Gilzean like fashion to head home at the Provost Road end. I can still see the header in my mind, looping over the German goalkeeper!

Cologne weren't out of it though and just over twenty minutes later they equalised. At half time, it was all square but the Germans were still in front on aggregate.

Then, a couple of objects appeared to be thrown at the interval and there seemed to be a bit of a minor scuffle further up the terracing so we decided to move round behind the T.C. Key end. With a bit of difficulty, we somehow managed to squeeze in down at the front right behind the goal that Dundee would be attacking in the second half. It was the first time since the European Cup match against Anderlecht (up that tree!) that I had watched a game from that end of Dens Park.

In the second half, the Germans went ahead with only half an hour to go, so we now needed to score three to go through. Cologne were no mugs and they really looked at that point as if they would go onto win it. They were so dominant but we kept plugging away. As time was going on, it appeared that German side were settling for the advantage that they had and started to sit deeper in defence. Dundee seemed to sense that all was not lost though and started to really apply some intense pressure on the German goal. Duncan then raised our hopes with an equaliser with around twenty minutes left on the clock. And then, with around *five* minutes to go, he equalised on aggregate. The whole place was going mad!

Donaldson, in Dundee's goal, then launched a huge kick deep into the Cologne half and in the "stramash" - as Arthur Montford (the well known commentator of the time) would say - that followed, Dundee looked to be awarded a penalty - but then, suddenly, the referee changed his mind!! Just what was all that about??? No one seemed to know. It really was bizarre.

Almost like the "Alamo", Dundee piled on more pressure. There was a huge goalmouth scramble and, from our view from behind the goal, twice it seemed as if the ball was going in, only for a German foot to deflect the ball to safety. The crowd were roaring the team on! Then, with almost the last attack of the game, after another almighty scramble in the box, the ball fell to Bobby Wilson and our right back became an unlikely hero when he thundered the ball into the net! It was pandemonium all around us! I have never ever seen such scenes of joy as I witnessed that evening. The memories of that match will last forever! What a great night! What a great team! The supporters that evening seemed to be a twelfth man for the team and I have never ever heard the fans before, or since, urge the team on so much as they did that night. At times, the crowd almost seemed to suck the ball into the Cologne goalmouth for Dundee!

But wait a minute. We can't get too carried away. After all, we are Dundee fans! On the following Saturday we travelled to Dens to see Dundee versus Morton in a League game. We lost 1-0. Back to reality with a bump. That's more like it, we thought!

November 13th 1971, Ibrox Stadium

Rangers 2 - 3 Dundee

My Dad had a thing about the Old Firm and he never really enjoyed going to games against Celtic or Rangers. It was okay when the game was at Dens but I think the hassle of finding parking spaces and of course, at that time, the lack of segregation at Ibrox and

Parkhead, put him off a bit, and so normally he would give these games a miss.

On this occasion though, I think that, like me, even though we had lost the week before to Morton, he was still on a bit of a high from the Cologne game so on a rather dull November day, we set out for Glasgow.

When we reached the stadium, with, again, no segregation in these days, we took our place in the main stand. Dundee, in white shirts and blue pants kicked off and, over the next fifteen minutes, turned in one of the most devastating performances that I was ever likely to witness. It was almost as if Rangers weren't even on the pitch as the white shirted Dark Blues took the Ibrox men apart with some scintillating football!

Within five minutes we were a goal up through the nonchalant skills of the underrated Alex Kinninmonth and, minutes later, Gordon Wallace made it two. Then, just on the fifteen minute mark, Davie Johnstone sent a rocket into the net to make it 3-0. Was this for real??? This team looked like the sons of Shankly out there!

Sometimes it is muted that you can score too early against the Old Firm giving them a chance to come back at you. However, we were enjoying the moment and some vociferous support from the back of the stand confirmed that we were not alone. Rangers though, ominously pulled one back just before half time and scored again about fifteen minutes after the break - but Dundee weren't finished. Duncan almost made it four when his well-struck shot from around twenty yards skimmed the far post before going harmlessly past. The pressure from Rangers was immense - but we stood firm. The final few minutes seemed to go on forever but at last, the final whistle blew. 3-2 the Dee!

Making our way back to the car, all we heard was, "Dundee, Dundee, Dundee," being chanted by happy Dundee fans. The journey home was a pleasant one to say the least, giving a peep on the horn to any car with victorious dark blue and white scarves billowing from their windows. It's always good to beat the Old Firm but even better on their own patch!

I could not wait for the next game. But when, oh when, will we ever learn? Being a Dundee fan is about turning up week in and week out, just not knowing what you are going to get.

November 20th 1971, Dens Park

Dundee 0 - 0 Clyde

Clyde were struggling second bottom of the league and, although we scored four against Cologne and three against Rangers at Ibrox, we couldn't register against Clyde! It finished 0-0. Yes, it was frustrating. We played almost all of the game in the Clyde half but we just couldn't get the ball in the net! "No wonder I'm losing my hair," was my Dad's comment as we left Dens Park!

Panic-o!

November 24th 1971, San Siro Stadium

UEFA Cup, 3rd Round

A.C. Milan 3 - 0 Dundee

The draw for the next round of the UEFA cup was made and we couldn't have drawn a more difficult tie. AC Milan. Yikes! Shades of 1963 when we met them in the European Cup surfaced.

In the first leg in Italy, Dundee played the Italians at their own game playing five at the back with Ian Phillip mopping up nearly everything behind a solid looking back four. Although we had lost an early goal, at half time, we were still very much in the match. However, another mix up between George Stewart and 'keeper Ally Donaldson (a common event at that time) saw the Italians go 2-0 ahead. Then a further on-target Milan strike before the end looked as if it had finished off any hopes Dundee had of progressing to the next stage in the competition.

December 8th 1971, Dens Park, UEFA Cup, 2nd leg

Dundee 2 - 0 AC Milan

In the build up to the game, we had won against Dunfermline and Airdrie but both these clubs were struggling in the Scottish League and it really wasn't a gauge as to what our form was going to be like in this second leg.

Dad and I travelled the road and the miles to Dundee yet again and took our place, this time, unusually for us, in the stand enclosure amongst the 16,000 crowd. The Italians started by defending defiantly. However, with around six minutes to go to half time, Duncan Lambie - who would go onto claim the man of the match - crossed and Gordon Wallace headed the ball into the net. 1-0. It was definitely "game on"!

In the second half it was one-way traffic as Dundee besieged the Milan goal. With only fifteen minutes left and urged on by a noisy home crowd, Lambie fired a shot against the post with Duncan following up, netting the rebound to make it 2-0! There were scenes of absolute joy all around us as visions of another "Cologne" became a possibility!

However, despite frantic Dundee pressure, the Italians held out for a 3-2 aggregate win. Gutted, is the only word that can be used to describe how I felt. We hadn't managed to get the equaliser our play deserved but I did manage to take great consolation from the fact that both Dad and myself could say, with all honesty, "Yes, we lost - but this time Dundee *did* play all the football!"

It had been a tremendous performance though against one of the giants of the European stage who, by their own admission, were mighty glad to hear the final whistle. Jock Stein, who took in the game from the main stand, said that it had been the best performance by a Scottish team in Europe since the "Lisbon Lions". So we were out of Europe but on reflection it is nice to be able to say that our record against A.C. Milan at Dens is quite impressive: played two and won two!

1971-72 turned out to be a decent season. Wonderful performances in Europe were matched by a double over Rangers; 3-2 at Ibrox and 2-0 at Dens. We scored six against United at Dens, taking three points out of a possible four against our neighbours from across the road, and we also whacked five in against Hearts at Tynecastle.

However, even though we finished in fifth place above United, for the second year running, we had been disappointing in the domestic cup competitions - although it can be argued that we more than made up for that in Europe!

We did finish the season with a trophy though, the Forfarshire Cup - again! Dad and I were there to see the white shirted 'Dee win 2-0 against United at Tannadice to lift the Cup. I know, it wasn't the Scottish Cup but when Doug Houston lifted the trophy on high, it was still a nice feeling!

Davie White had now taken over at Dens (January 1972) and much respected coach Jim Mclean had by this time slotted in as manager of United. Dad made the comment that in the recent Forfarshire Cup Final, it had been the first time that he had seen United play such good football. Hmm......little did we know!

So I hung my scarf in the wardrobe, envisioning waving it in the air next season when Dundee would lift the Scottish Cup. Well, I could dream.

Chapter 17

Consolation?

Season 1972-73 started at Firs Park, home of East Stirlingshire. The League Cup sections that season, in attempt to perhaps get a little romance back into the competition for the smaller clubs, saw the First Division teams seeded and two First and two Second Division clubs make up each section. Dundee found themselves with East Stirling and Clyde from the Second Division and Motherwell from the First.

I had completed, without mishap, two weeks of rigorous full time training at the University of Stirling where the SFA were holding their coaching courses. During the course, one of the coaches had apparently recommended me to both Alloa Athletic and Hearts and, although I was flattered that I had impressed enough to be recommended to a club of Heart's stature, at the time I felt - on reflection, wrongly - that I might be better off trying to get back to playing at a lower level and signed for the "Wasps" on a monthly contract to prove my fitness. Unfortunately however, I was signed too late to play in the opening game and therefore, as a “consolation”, travelled to Falkirk with my Dad for Dundee’s opening League Cup fixture.

August 12th 1972, Firs Park

East Stirling 2 - 8 Dundee

There was only around 1,500 in the Shire’s tiny ground - most of them from Dundee - and it turned into a walkover by a Dundee side that just oozed quality. John Duncan got his name in lights with a five-goal spree and singles from Bobby Robinson, Jimmy Wilson and an own goal by Stein of East Stirling, completed a miserable opening day for the Second Division side.

It could be argued that East Stirling were hardly a bench mark on which to assess Dundee’s prospects for the season but it was still a mighty impressive performance by the white shirted Dark Blues.

My Game:

August 16th 1972, Recreation Park

Alloa Athletic 4 - 3 Albion Rovers

On the following Wednesday, whilst Dundee were taking on Clyde at Dens Park, I made my debut for Alloa. It was my first competitive senior game for almost four seasons but I felt ready and confident. I was playing up through the middle that evening and remember well my marker getting too tight with me as I went to receive a pass. I dummied the ball, it then hit off the defender and I got the rebound and slammed the ball into the net from a tight angle! What a feeling! It turned out to be real classic of a match, with Alloa eventually running out 4-3 winners! I was pretty tired and sore after so long out of the game but driving home I felt so happy that I had proved to myself - and others - that I could still cut it at Senior level.

Later, I learned that Dundee had won 2-1 so it was a very good day for me all round! The manager at Alloa, Dan Mclinden (ex-Dunfermline) and ex-Celtic goalkeeper coach, Frank Connor (who went on to become assistant manager of Celtic), said to me after the game that they were delighted with my performance. I had waited so long to get back playing at senior level and now it seemed that all my hard work was paying off. To play well was great but to score as well, was icing on the cake. I was back, I thought. I felt really sharp and, despite not having played at senior level for nearly four years, I felt very comfortable and indeed felt that I could actually go on to perhaps play at a higher level.

The following Saturday I played against Dumbarton in a 0-0 draw and the manager told me that I was the best player on the pitch. “What was the score with Dundee?” I asked, after I had showered.

“Won 3-1,” somebody in the dressing room shouted. Another good day - apart from the fact that I had tweaked my groin! The next day I was having difficulty even getting in and out of my car and thought that I would be struggling to make the match against Brechin City on the following Wednesday.

August 23rd 1972, Shawfield Stadium, League Cup

Clyde 0 - 1 Dundee

I wasn't fit for the midweek game at Brechin so on the Wednesday evening, Dad and I made our way to Shawfield to see Dundee take on Clyde - another "consolation" for me. Ian Philips scored the only goal of the game but Dundee won more comfortably than the score suggests. Clyde were in the Second Division at the time and, roared on by the home crowd, they had a lot of the game but it was evident that Dundee had the class. Although the score was only 1-0, I felt that Dundee actually played well within themselves and, if the need had arisen, they could have upped a gear and perhaps won by a greater margin.

At Alloa, the games were coming thick and fast and having won our League Cup section we were drawn to play First Division Ayr United over two legs in the next round. Ayr, managed at the time by Ally Mcleod, had just beaten Rangers 2-1 on the Saturday in the League and had ex 'Dee George McLean in their side.

In the first leg at Alloa, on a Monday evening, we drew 0-0. I nearly won it for the "Wasps" though, with a volley that rebounded from their keeper's chest, with him not knowing much about it! In the second leg however, and *only two days* later, having not played for almost four seasons, my body was crying out for a rest. Somerset Park was never an easy place to get a result but even more so at that time as Ayr were a decent top league side and were sitting in the top half of the First Division. We won though, 1-0!

We scored early in the second half from a breakaway and for the rest of the game we were camped in our own half. I found myself in our own penalty box helping to defend more often than I was in the opposition penalty area. Willie McCulloch, who would go on to win a runner up Scottish Cup medal in later years with Airdrie, got the all important goal.

Although I had played well enough, I was beginning to recognise that there were signs that I was asking far too much of myself, and the sharpness and confidence that I had taken into my early games was waning a bit. On reflection, two games a week were far too much for me after such a long time out. In that particular week, I had been asked to play two games in three days against top league full time opposition and in that game, however, I had some more bad luck, injury wise.

I badly hurt my big toe and the trainer suspected it was broken - but I continued to play on. I missed the next game but after a pain killing injection - not to be recommended! - I was back for the derby against Stirling Albion, only a week later. I was, of course, nowhere near fit and shouldn't even have been on the pitch but Frank Connor, our coach, kept on at me. "You can do it wee man!" he kept saying, and of course, as I was desperate to play, I took to the field with my big toe all strapped up and covered in cotton wool.

Bucking Hell!

But then bad luck strikes again. Buck McGarry - who will be remembered for his time with St Johnstone - after jumping for a ball at a corner, landed - yes, you guessed it - right on my sore toe! What are the chances??!! Buck, as some of you may remember, was no lightweight, the exact opposite in fact. The pain was excruciating but, desperately wanting to do well and win a contract, I carried on. But boy, I was in agony and it was, in hindsight, a big, *big* mistake. But even worse was to follow.

The following week at training I seemed to jar my back and later that evening I felt really bad pains down my leg. The pain was really bad by the weekend and, as my toe was still sore, I had another jag but told the Boss that I couldn't possibly play against East Stirling on the Saturday. On the Friday evening before the game however, Frank was on the phone cajoling me to play and persuaded me to sit on the bench as a substitute. "You can come on and win it for us wee man!" was his parting comment that evening.

Stupidly, I conceded and the next day I came on with about half an hour left. I was limping when I was warming up and told myself that I was daft to concede to Frank's persuasion but I went on and saw the game out. We won 2-0, I think. On the Sunday morning, I could hardly get out of bed. I was sent to hospital where it was discovered that I had two slipped discs. I sure was a sorry sight! I was limping on the right side because of my sore toe and limping on my left because of my slipped discs!

I had two exploratory operations but the surgeon advised that operating could make it worse so, very disappointingly, I found that my long hard slog to fitness and my quest to play again at senior level was to no avail. I was on a monthly contract and so, of course, it wasn't renewed. I had to hang my boots up at the ripe old age of twenty-five.

I am not ashamed to say that I shed quite a few tears. Sometime later I was asked if I fancied a trial with Dunfermline. I trained with the "Pars" for a few weeks but felt that my fitness was lacking and my back hurt a bit and I just couldn't face going through all the agony again and so decided that enough was enough.

What now, I thought? Well, I was in my final year at the Victoria College in Glasgow and I harboured thoughts of getting back into football by doing Sports Therapy, along with coaching, so I would just have to wait and see what unfolded. One thing was for sure though; having worked so hard to get back into senior football, not being involved at all was not an option for me, as I knew from my previous experience that I would miss it too much.

In the meantime, it was back to the cupboard to seek out my dark blue and white scarf! My "consolation"! Playing again had been great and nothing could ever replace that but following the 'Dee was something that I was again starting to look forward to - and what a game to start with.

September 23rd 1972, Dens Park

Dundee 2 - 0 Celtic

Celtic were sweeping all before them and were in the seventh season of their famous nine in a row championship successes. However, Dundee looked up for the challenge and scored twice in the opening fifteen minutes, through Ian Scott and young John Gray - who was now challenging for a starting berth. We waited for the onslaught from Celtic but it never came and, in the second half, we were much the better side and held on comfortably to win 2-0.

The next game that I can remember attending was also against Celtic in the quarter final of the league Cup which was played over two legs, the first of which was at Dens Park.

October 11th 1972, Dens Park

League Cup Quarter Final, 1st leg

Dundee 1 - 0 Celtic

Dad used to say that when he switched the engine on in the car, it would automatically make its way to Dens Park. Considering that we had to drive over a hundred miles round trip to get to a home match, we must have driven thousands of miles following our beloved Dark Blues, and that night we were on our way again!

Celtic, according to the National Press, were, "Up for it." Still stinging from the 2-0 reverse that they had endured only two weeks previously, they were in no mood to concede another defeat - but what they didn't bank on, was that we were "up for it" as well.

The atmosphere was terrific that night and it wasn't long before the 'Dee went ahead with Gordon Wallace finding the back of the net. 1-0. Celtic then really turned up the heat and we had our hearts in our mouths on several occasions as the "hoops" piled on the pressure. However, our 'keeper Thomson Allen was immense that evening and was our star performer - and he needed to be! It finished 1-0 but could have been a completely different story!

22,000 had attended that mid week match, which was almost 4,000 up on the earlier meeting between the two teams and Dundee were being quoted as being the only team in Scotland who could give

Celtic a run for their money. However, although in the near future there would be many dramatic contests between the two sides, Celtic always seemed to find that bit extra in the numerous semi-final ties and stopped the 'Dee getting to several cup finals.

Nov 1st 1972, Celtic Park, League Cup, 2nd leg

Celtic 3 - 2 Dundee (aggregate 3-3)

Celtic started the game rampant and went ahead early on and quickly went 2-0 ahead (2-1 up on aggregate) but, just when it looked to be all over in the first half, Gordon Wallace pulled a goal back for us, levelling the score on aggregate.

In the second half, nearly 40,000 Celtic fans roared their team on and saw their favourites score a third. This time, it was surely all over, we suspected. However, unexpectedly late in the game, Dad and I found ourselves on our feet again, cheering wildly when Jocky Scott jinked passed a couple of defenders and unleashed a spectacular drive into the net from well outside the box - much to the disgust of the Celtic fans around us. What a goal though! We could win this, we thought.

But the clock beat us. Full time came around with no more scoring - it was into extra time. Heart in the mouth stuff followed as Celtic piled on the pressure again - but we stood firm. It finished 3-3 on aggregate. What a game. We lived to fight another day!

November 4th 1972, Dens Park

Dundee 1 - 1 Rangers

Our next match was back to League business against the other half of the old firm, Rangers, at Dens Park. I have to say that I was worried about this game and, as we drove to Dens, my Dad expressed the same concern. Dundee had just played two hours of football only seventy-two hours previously and we both feared that another high tempo game against one of the old firm might just be too much for us.

However, we needn't have worried. We, amongst a crowd of 20,000, witnessed a real classic of a match. Gordon Wallace (just how he never won a full cap is beyond me) put us in front from a classic Dundee counter attack with Gordon, alert as ever, sneaking in at the back post to score. We were on our feet, cheering wildly! What an atmosphere! Over 40,000 at Celtic Park on Wednesday and another bumper crowd here at Dens. We could get used to this! Rangers then dampened the mood slightly by equalising however, through a solo effort by Alfie Conn.

In the second half we were subjected to a lot of pressure but looked dangerous on the break, and we nearly won it at the death but the Ranger's defence scrambled the ball to safety and it finished 1-1. But we were proud of our team though. Rangers were strong and physical but most of the classy football had come from Dundee - again!

But just as we thought that a title challenge could be on, the following Saturday in the League match at Gayfield, we did the usual Dundee thing - we lost. Arbroath 2, Dundee 1. It was Jocky Scott of all people, who scored an own goal! That day it was a long and dreary journey home and overnight we had gone from looking like title challengers, sitting on the coat tails of the Old Firm to around fifth, in a tight and pretty competitive League.

Our next game however, before meeting Celtic at Hampden in the League Cup replay, was a little more comforting. It was St Johnstone at Dens and the “Saintees” were put to the sword in a convincing 3-0 drubbing of the Perth side. Duncan, Robinson and Houston were on the score sheet and so we left Dens full of hope for the up and coming cup tie in Glasgow.

November 30th 1972

League Cup Quarter Final Replay, Hampden Park

Celtic 4 - 1 Dundee

We stood in the old North Enclosure, almost exactly where we had stood in the 1964 Cup final against the other half of the Old firm. The game started really positively for us with Dundee opening the scoring through Jocky Scott. Then it all turned sour. Celtic turned up the pressure and, unbelievably, we lost *four* goals before half time. But credit where credit's due; they were devastating in the last half hour of the first half. Against any other side, Dundee's performance would probably been good enough but it really *was* all over now, we felt.

In the second half, Dundee gave as good as they got but the three goal deficit was always going to be too much. To be honest, the game was over at half time - and everybody knew it. As we made our way out of the stadium, surrounded by Celtic fans, my Dad repeated his famous saying, "We must be daft!"

Following our League Cup exit, we made the long journey to Ayr, where I had tasted victory earlier in the season with Alloa. The 'Dee, still looking a bit leg weary from their efforts against Celtic, went down 2-1. However, not to worry too much as that was to kick start a five game unbeaten run which saw us take full points from East Fife, Partick Thistle, Hearts and Motherwell, and a point at Falkirk. But disappointingly, we lost at Aberdeen on New Years Day. I hated when we lost on New Year's Day. Talk about spoiling the party atmosphere!

Our next game was against Dundee United at Dens Park. Earlier that season, I had taken my wife Elma to the Forfarshire Cup Final against United at Tannadice. It was on a Wenesday evening, which I remember clearly, only because the weather was so dire that night - but we were worse - we lost 4-0!

January 6th 1973, Dens Park

Dundee 3 - 0 Dundee United

So it was with some feeling of revenge that Dad and I, accompanied by the Mortimers, went to Dens to take in yet another Tayside derby. In order to keep up our challenge near the top of the table, we really needed to win this one as we had lost the New Year's Day clash at Pittodrie, 3-1 to Aberdeen.

We all agreed going up in the car that if Dundee played to their potential, we would win. Simple as that! And for once, our confidence didn't come back to bite us in the backside.

We did play exactly as we could and two goals from John Duncan and a surprise counter from Doug Houston ensured that we took the points in a 3-0 going-on-six victory. We elected to sit in the main stand for this one and it was the first time for a long time that I can remember feeling quite relaxed at a derby match. Dundee played their football and had United chasing shadows for much of the game. It sure was a happy car on the road home!

Consolation?

It was The Scottish Cup that was going to be our only chance of glory however, as we had fallen way behind the Old Firm in the league.

February 3rd 1973, East End Park

Scottish Cup, 3rd Round

Dunfermline Athletic 0 - 3 Dundee

The Dark Blues were drawn against Dunfermline at East End in the Third Round. However, even though the "Pars" were in the Second Division at the time, it was still a tricky draw - but we came through unscathed. Before a crowd of over 10,000, the Second Division side started strongly but Dundee resisted their opening onslaught. Urged on by a vociferous visiting support, the Dark Blues soon showed their undoubted class and goals from Wilson, Duncan and Jocky Scott were too much for the home side to overcome. We triumphed in a 3-0 victory!

February 20th 1973, Stair Park

Scottish Cup, 4th Round

Stranraer 2 - 9 Dundee

In the games leading up to the cup clash at Stranraer, we were unbeaten but our form had not been great. We had squeezed passed Dumbarton by only 2-1 at Dens, before earning a point in another unconvincing performance against Airdrie in a 1-1 draw at Broomfield.

However, a goal glut at Stranraer in Round Four saw John Duncan score four with Gordon Wallace netting a hat-trick in a 9-2 win! Goals from Doug Houston and Ian Scott completed the scoring. Games against lower league sides can be tricky as these sides have nothing to lose and they can be potential "banana skins" for the bigger teams but, on this occasion, the gap in class was too much for Stranraer. Dundee, clinical in their finishing, ran out easy winners.

March 17th 1973, Links Park
Scottish Cup Quarter Final
Montrose 1 - 4 Dundee

The "gods" were, for once, kind to us, pairing us with an away draw at Second Division Montrose. Much had been made of the fact that sometimes the bigger clubs can come a cropper if their attitude is suspect in these sort of matches and a record crowd of nearly 9,000 turned out to see if a surprise could be on the cards. The match had a bit more spice to it than the clash with Stranraer as Montrose saw this as a bit of a derby match and a chance of glory. However, although the Second Division side were gutsy, they were no match for the classy Dens men and goals from Wallace, Duncan and two from Jocky Scott, saw us safely through in a convincing 4-1 win.

Then, surprise, surprise, in the semi final we drew Celtic - again!

April 7th 1973, Hampden Park

Scottish Cup Semi Final

Celtic 0 - 0 Dundee

After their epic League Cup games with Celtic earlier in the season, there was great anticipation going into the match at Hampden. Unfortunately, a dose of the 'flu prevented me going to the match, and so I listened in at home to the radio; mentally and maybe even spiritually, kicking every ball. Every time the commentator raised his voice it seemed as if Celtic were going to score. I couldn't bear to listen anymore and, cowardly perhaps, switched the radio off and went out to the garden for some fresh air.

We drew 0-0. When the result came through, in a way, it was almost like a win as most people expected us to lose.

April 11th 1973, Hampden Park

Scottish Cup Semi Final, Replay

Full Time: Celtic 0 - 0 Dundee

Extra Time: Celtic 3 - 0 Dundee

In the replay, I was still off work and unable to attend the game, so again, I was glued to the radio. Listening was absolute torture. Full time came and it was 0-0. There was still hope! However, in extra time, we crumbled and lost three goals. I was devastated. According to reports, in the normal playing time, we had quite a few chances to win it but didn't take them. Such is life when you support the 'Dee.

The season came to an end with Celtic winning the league with a point to spare over Rangers. Hibs finished third, twelve points behind with Dundee finishing fifth, equal on points with Aberdeen, two behind third place Hibs - but - importantly, for me - above United, for the third season running! But we were a long way behind Champions Celtic, fourteen to be exact.

A semi final Scottish Cup place for the second successive season was our lot. However, it had at least been an interesting season. But could we go one better next season and win a trophy?

Chapter 18

How Could I Miss This?!

The season 1973-74 started in earnest for me with a mid week tussle with Partick Thistle at Dens Park on August 22nd. We had won our opening League Cup match at Perth, beating St Johnstone 1-0 but I was on holiday and missed that one. However, I cut short my touring holiday in the North of Scotland (I wasn't Mr. Popular!) to make the long trip to Dundee for the match against Thistle - and it was worth it. We won 4-0! Sure glad I didn't miss that one!

Over all the years that I had supported Dundee, they had always been famed for their sophisticated football and, as mentioned before, it was a great consolation at times, even when they lost, to see the team pass the opposition off the park.

I always used my Dad's seemingly favourite cliché of, "But Dundee played the football." And in the main, if I'm honest, this phrase was justified, as there were few teams who could surpass Dundee for passing and chic football. Enter Dutch side Twente Enschede.

September 19th 1973, Dens Park, UEFA Cup

Dundee 1 - 3 Twente Enschede

This was the night that Dundee lost their proud record of being unbeaten at home in European competition, losing 3-1 to the Dutch side. In truth, we were totally played off the park. The Dutch were still relatively unknown as a major force in football (although at the next World Cup they would show just how much they had improved) but clearly they had worked very hard at improving their technique. I have always been a scholar of pure football and I could not help but applaud the Dutch team off the pitch. Simply put, the Dutch were in a different league. Much had been written in the press about the Dutch National side attaching themselves to what was termed "total football", but if this was an example of that philosophy, then world football was about to see a change for the better. Twente controlled the game from start to finish; their full backs seemed to be attacking as much their forwards and whenever they lost possession - which wasn't often - *every* man seemed to be a defender. Defensive players were just as comfortable on the ball as forwards and the mid fielders were as efficient in their defensive work as they were in attack - and the team's man-to-man possession football was a joy to behold.

After the 3-1 defeat at Dens, a second leg 4-2 reverse in Holland followed, which meant that Dundee were despatched early from the European scene. 4-2 across in Holland was to be honest, not a bad result, for make no mistake, although this was a very good Dundee side, they couldn't live with the Dutch team. I think that defeat hurt most, not just because we lost - but because we had indeed been outclassed. Ouch! Never thought that I would ever say that so blatantly!

There was still the League Cup though and the 'Dee scraped through against Dunfermline, drawing the second leg 2-2 at Dens but winning 5-4 on aggregate over the two games.

September 15th 1973, Dens Park

Dundee 0 - 1 Dundee United

Up to the week before the game against Twente, Dad and I had only missed two games, and were really encouraged by all the team's performances so far. We had walloped Falkirk 4-0, drawn at Aberdeen and defeated Dunfermline 3-2 in the League Cup. However, against United we never seemed to get a rub of the green and, despite being the better side (I'm not being biased, honest!), we lost 1-0.

This started a losing streak; we then went seven games in a row without a win. I don't know why we always seemed to dominate most Derby matches at that time but still end up losing! We were a much better side than United but psychologically it seemed, on occasion, that our friends from across the road had the Indian sign on us.

The Derby reverse seemed to kick off a real bad patch for us and although we drew 2-2 at Tynecastle, defeats from East Fife, Partick Thistle and a 1-0 home loss to Celtic followed.

Still keeping faith though, we made the long trip to Arbroath and saw our team win a tricky fixture 4-2. Games against Arbroath - whilst no big deal for our supporters - were probably the highlight of the season for Arbroath fans. The atmosphere in the trim little stadium was always good whenever we visited and it was no different on this occasion. Our class however, was too much for the plucky "red lichties" and goals from Wallace, Bobby Wilson, Scott and Robinson ensured that the points headed down the road to Dens.

That result seemed to turn the corner for us and we won the next four in a row before losing 2-1 to a strong Hibs side at Easter Road. Then, in the second leg of the League Cup Quarter Final at Dens, we squeezed passed Clyde on aggregate with a 2-2 draw. We missed that game but had been at Shawfield for the first leg where we won 1-0 - thanks to a John Duncan goal! Despite our indifferent form, we were in the Semi Final of the League Cup! Could we get to a Hampden *final*?!

At 60 Ochil Street, Tillicoultry, it was all very quiet as we listened in to the draw for the semi. Rangers versus Celtic came out first - great news! No Celtic in the semis!! It was the first time for some while that we had not drawn Celtic at this stage of the Domestic Cup competitions. We were instead drawn against Kilmarnock and, with no disrespect to Killie, they were a Second Division club at the time and we felt we were clear favourites for a final place.

However, being a Dundee fan I really should have known better than to consider ourselves favourites to win any game of football - no matter who it was against!! In the build up to the semi final we were murdered 5-1 at Dens by Dunfermline, who finished third bottom of the league that season. Here we go again, I thought.

Finally In The Final!

November 28th 1973, Hampden Park

Scottish League Cup, Semi Final

Dundee 1 - 0 Kilmarnock

Now what should be remembered at this point is that the whole of the country was involved in an energy crisis. There was a National Miner's strike and most of the country was on a three-day working week. There was petrol rationing, a 50mph speed limit to restrict the amount of fuel being used, and no floodlit games were allowed. Along with all that, on the night of the match, the weather was horrendous. The rain battered down all day and so there was just no way that we could get to Hampden that night. It would have to be the radio.

I made my way to my Dad's house and listened to the game. That evening, the floodlights were powered by a generator and were apparently nowhere near as powerful as the normal Hampden lights and, because of the strike, fewer than 5,000 fans managed to attend, which made for quite a surreal atmosphere.

When the game kicked off, the conditions appeared to favour the Ayrshire side as the surface did nothing for Dundee's short passing game. Killie were belittling our "favourites" tag and put us under a bit of early pressure - but it was still 0-0 at half time. Early in the second half though, to great jubilation in the Caproni household, Tommy Gemmell put us in front! We assumed that this goal would signal more attacking from the favourites but it was Killie who kept on surging forward, looking for the equaliser. Late in the match our hearts were in our mouths on several occasions as the Second Division side went for broke. However, Tommy Gemmell was playing a real captain's part and, not content with just scoring our goal, he broke the Kilmarnock hearts with two goal line clearances in the dying minutes. "Blow your whistle ref and put us out of our misery!" Dad and I screamed at the radio. Seconds later the final whistle finally blew. We were in the Scottish League Cup Final! At last!!!!

Time For Some Therapy

Away from following Dundee, I got the results of the recent examination I sat at the Victoria College and learned that I had passed. That same week, I read that Stirling Albion, the club for whom I used to play, were looking for someone to join the backroom staff and, although I loved following the 'Dee every week, the lure of getting back into professional football was too strong, so I applied for the job. Nothing could replace playing but being involved as Fitness and Remedial Sports Therapist coupled with doing a bit of coaching with the young players was something that I always wanted to do.

Bob Shankly was the General Manager at Stirling, and the team manager was Frank Beattie, who used to play for Kilmarnock. They both interviewed me and immediately offered me the job. I took up my new position the day after Dundee's semi final win.

Shanks Again

Mention the name Bob Shankly, or Shanks, as he was more commonly known, to any former player, and there will be few, if any, who would have anything other than good things to say. He was a man who was as honest as the day was long. So honest, in fact, that he could be brutal with it and, as recorded earlier in this book, if you didn't like what he said, then that was tough!

I worked with Bob Shankly for over twelve years and listening to the man was an education. Simplicity was his philosophy. Modern day jargon was not for him and the stories about him recorded earlier in this book are only a few of many I could tell!

Shanks - to all Dundee supporters - is a legend and, of course, was manager of the side when they won the League Championship. He also took that great side to within inches of immortality the following season, when they reached the semi final of the European Cup, losing to the eventual winners, AC Milan.

Shanks was a one off and when it was announced that he had collapsed and died at a meeting at the SFA at Glasgow, the whole of Scottish football was shaken to it's very roots. I was driving home from Falkirk at the time when I received a call from George Peebles, who was assistant manager at the Albion, to tell me that Shanks had died. I was absolutely shocked and devastated. I, probably more than most at the club, missed Shanks a lot. I was always first at the ground on both match and training days and we always had a good "natter" together about whatever was happening in the game both at Stirling Albion and beyond. Whenever I take my seat in Dens Park, I cannot help but glance up at the "BOB SHANKLY STAND". I am proud to have worked with Bob Shankly the manager, but prouder still, that I knew Bob Shankly, the man.

Victorious And Glorious!

December 15th 1972, Hampden Park

Scottish League Cup Final

Dundee 1-0 Celtic

&

December 15th 1972, Starks Park

Scottish League Division 2

Raith Rovers v Stirling Albion

When I woke that morning, my first thought was that I just couldn't believe that I was missing the game. Dundee were in a Cup Final - and I wouldn't be there!!

To accommodate for any possible extra time, the Scottish League Cup Final was scheduled to kick off at 1.30pm. The weather was horrendous and there was severe doubt as to whether the game would even go ahead. Snow, slush and water lay on the Hampden pitch and both managers expressed concern, indicating that they would prefer the game to be rescheduled. However, after a late inspection, the game went ahead - in front of only just less than 30,000 fans.

Stirling Albion's kick off at Kirkcaldy was scheduled for 2.00pm. We arrived at just after 12.30pm and learned that, because of worsening conditions, there was to be a late pitch inspection and, after what seemed like an *eternity*, our game was postponed. I could not believe it. Dundee were in the Cup Final at Hampden and our game was now called off! My first thoughts that I had are actually unprintable!!

We got back on the bus and the Boss phoned East End Park, where Hibs were visitors to Dunfermline, to see if we could get access to the game. As we approached Dunfermline, the Dundee game had started and was on the bus radio but I didn't want to draw too much attention to the fact that this was life or death to me! We arrived at East End Park with the teams having played around ten minutes. I still couldn't get my head round the fact that I was sitting in East End Park watching Dunfermline play Hibs when Dundee were playing in a Cup Final at Hampden! I was numb. Whilst in the lounge at half time, I learned that it was still 0-0 at Hampden.

Later, with around ten minutes to go until full time, we made our way from East End Park. I still hadn't heard the latest score at Hampden but, just as I was about to climb on to the team bus, our kit manager at the time, a really nice old guy called George Rilley, said to me, "I heard Dundee won the cup." Aghhhhhh!!!!!!!!! I wanted to jump up and down!! I replied as nonchalantly as I could however, "Ahem, are you certain?"

"Aye," he replied, "1-0."

My excitement nearly bubbling over, I took my seat on the bus and the driver switched on the radio, just in time for me to catch an interview with, "The VICTORIOUS Dundee skipper, Tommy Gemmell," was how the interviewer described him. We HAD won the cup! It *was* real!!! We arrived back at Annfield Park and after a few minutes that it took to leave the bus - which felt like a lifetime - I was in my car driving home, where I could finally let loose!! It was twelve miles from Stirling Albion's ground to my home and I sang the praises of my team all the way!! In the evening, I made my way to my father's house to watch the highlights.

The Hampden pitch had been snow covered when the action began and then heavy rain developed later, so the players had to splash through surface water throughout the second half.

But it was a game in which neither side really dominated. In the second half, however, Celtic had done slightly more of the attacking but Dundee were dangerous on the break and a Stewart header for Dundee in the seventy-fourth minute almost broke the deadlock. Then, with only thirteen minutes left, Dundee finally went ahead with a brilliant goal from striker Gordon Wallace. The Dark Blues were awarded a free kick about forty yards from goal on the right and Wilson's ball went to Gordon, who let it drop from his chest before pivoting and sending a twelve yard shot to the left hand corner of the Celtic goalkeeper's net! Whilst watching the game on TV in the evening Dad and I both cheered wildly when Gordon Wallace netted his legendary goal!

Celtic's reply was immediate and intensive. They roared into attack and, late in the game, Dundee hearts were in their mouths as a header from ex 'Dee Stevie Murray swept only inches wide. But Dundee held out for a glorious victory! Wallace's brilliant goal was enough to take the cup to Dens for the first time since 1952. What a night to remember!

It had been eleven long seasons since Dundee had won a trophy, and although we had come close on several occasions we always seemed to miss out on the big prize, but not this time. For the record, the players who brought the trophy to Dens Park were as follows: Allan, Wilson, Gemmell, Ford, Stewart, Philip, Duncan,

Snapped in the Stranraer dressing room after clinching promotion in 1977.

That's me on the extreme left, behind Shanks, after the Albion had won promotion at Stranraer.

Dundee forever! Keeping it in the family - my three children in their Dundee strips in the eighties. Left to right: Michael, Elizabeth and Mark.

Robinson, Wallace, J. Scott and Lambie. Substitutes: I. Scott and Johnstone.

It was a great pity that circumstances had dictated that fewer than 30,000 attended and the weather had spoiled what could have been a classic. My dream was always to be at Hampden to see a Dundee captain lift a cup aloft in triumph. HOW, OH HOW, DID I MISS THAT???!!! Maybe, hopefully, they will do it again.........?

Chapter 19

Dens Park:

Our Theatre Of Dreams

Whenever I happened to visit the city of Dundee on business (I eventually worked as a Director with a health and safety company) - nothing to do with football - I always made a point of, by hook or by crook, paying a visit to Dens Park. I would park my car on a nearby street at lunchtime and just sit and look at the stadium. What wonderful memories that old stadium has given me, and thousands like me.

I will be forever grateful to my Dad, who passed away in 1991, for introducing me to Dundee Football Club. From the age of seven, I trailed the country with him, following our beloved Dark Blues and suffering many a disappointment. But as Dad used to always say, "We have our moments."

“Moments” we certainly did have - and I cherish them. Victories over the cream of Europe, triumphs over the “Old Firm”, and wonderful, classy football, that was the envy of the Scottish game.

Dens Park. The first time I ever heard a radio report on a game there, the reporter referred to it as, “Dreary and dismal Dens Park.” It might have had something to do with the weather at the time and maybe even the game itself but, over the years for me, Dens Park has been anything but dismal or indeed dreary.

The memories flood thick and fast:

My first league game that I attended at Dens against Hearts, a 3-3 draw with Alan Cousin scoring a wonderful equaliser against the then Champions; the match against Anderlecht in the European Cup, when Dad and I watched from up a tree behind the TC Key end; Cologne in the FAIRS/UEFA Cup, and the famous fight back that saw Dundee go through with a last gasp goal from Bobby Wilson; scoring six against United and regular victories over Rangers and Celtic!

To have seen in the flesh, wonderful players like Doug Cowie, Alan Gilzean, Alan Cousin, Gordon Smith, Ian Ure, Charlie Cooke, Gordon Wallace, Jocky Scott and, of course more recently, Claudio

Canniggia and Georgi Nemsadze, was a joy to behold. Their quality, we aren't likely to ever see again.

Great goalkeepers like Bill Brown, Pat Liney, Bert Slater, Ally Donaldson and Thomson Allan whose performances between the sticks are memories etched in my mind forever.

However, it would not be Dundee if everything went according to plan all the time - and sometimes, that was a good thing. The unpredictability, Dad used to say, is part of the fun in supporting the Dark Blues. When we were being tipped in the press to lose to the Old Firm, Dad used to say to his work colleagues, "Don't say I didn't warn you," predicting that Dundee might just claim a victory. And in the circumstances when Dundee did pip a win, what better than to gloat the following Monday! It worked the other way as well of course - and many a sore heart we had!!

Although we, at the moment - and I stress, *at the moment* (2009) - are no longer the force that we once were, I still really look forward to a Saturday. I am so fortunate to have seen Dundee arguably at the best time in their history, which is confirmed when I speak to my pal, with whom I travel to away games, Bruce Porter. Bruce is twenty years younger than me and perhaps has only the Bonetti era as his best footballing memories and names like Gilzean and Cousin are indeed just that - names.

But in my experience, football goes in cycles. Look at Kilmarnock: for several seasons they languished in the Second Division but are now are a respectable SPL club. And Motherwell, who like us, experienced administration but recently played in the UEFA cup. And not forgetting our "friends" across the road of course, United. For the first eighty years of their existence, they were also-rans in the city of Dundee, never mind Scotland. So all is not lost and with the board appointment of millionaire Calum Melville and an ambitious hard working board lead by Chairman Bob Brannon, hopefully, we will shortly once again be one of Scotland's elite.

On many occasions however, when I have found myself making my way out of the stadium after a disappointing result and facing a long and depressing journey home, I can almost hear my father's words, echoing in my ear. "We must be daft!" I think it's true. I, and many thousands like me, must indeed be just that.

But we must remember that following the "Dee" is a marathon, not a sprint, and you have to - even in the darkest hour - learn to keep the faith! As the song goes, "Although on occasion defeat we must know, we will rise up again and defeat every foe!"

C'mon the 'Dee'!!

ABOUT THE AUTHOR

Peter Caproni played at senior professional level with Stirling Albion and Alloa Athletic and, although illness then injury cut short his career as a player, he spent over thirty years in the professional game.

As a qualified Fitness and Sports Therapist, he worked on the back room staff of six senior clubs including Dundee F.C. In his two and half seasons at Dens Park under, initially, Jocky Scott, to be followed in quick succession by Dave Smith and Gordon Wallace, Peter established a coaching class for Dundee FC at Stirling University. Peter supported first, Bobby Glennie, then the late Bert Slater and finally Billy Kirkwood, on a Saturday with the reserve team.

Before taking up his part time role with Dundee, Peter spent seventeen seasons at Stirling Albion. After Dundee were relegated in 1989-90 the reserve team started to play their games in mid week which was inconvenient and clashed with work commitments, so he accepted Alex Smith's invitation to take up a similar position at Aberdeen.

Peter spent two seasons helping Willie Millar with the reserves before being invited back to Stirling Albion by John Brogan to take up the position of Youth Development Officer and establish the Albion youth policy. Two of the youth players signed by Peter were later sold on for around £200,000, a significant sum of money for a club like Stirling Albion.

After five seasons, Peter joined Eamonn Bannon's Falkirk F.C. as u/18 Youth Coach then had a season at East Fife coaching their u/21 side during Jimmy Bone's tenure. When Jimmy Bone moved on to take up the position of assistant to Jocky Scott at Dens, Peter took up a scouting position with Luton Town.

Peter has worked with fourteen different managers including the late, great Bob Shankly, for twelve years at Stirling Albion.

Away from football Peter was a Director of a company selling Health and Safety products and now runs his own Sports Injury Clinic in Sauchie, Clackmannanshire, aptly called, The Treatment Room.

During his time in professional football, Peter's love of Dundee Football Club remained, and on retiring from the game in 1999, he has seldom missed a game home or away and is a season ticket holder at Dens Park.